30 Years of Fine Publications of *China's Tibet*

PEOPLE ON THE QINGHAI-TIBET PLATEAU

edited by
CHINA'S TIBET MAGAZINE

THE CHINA TIBETOLOGY PUBLISHING HOUSE

PREFACE

RECORDING THE NEW ERA AND SHARING STORIES OF MODERN-DAY TIBET

—Written in Celebration of the 30th Anniversary of the Publication of *China's Tibet*

70 years ago, the People's Republic of China declared its sovereignty and achieved national independence. 60 years ago, Tibet was liberated from its oppressive feudalistic rule and entered a new, democratic era. Though only five dozen years have passed, truly a blink of an eye from the perspective of world history, thanks to the Communist Party of China, Tibet has never in its existence experienced such a widespread and profound transformation among its people. Over a million serfs, essentially slaves, were emancipated. Today, they and their descendants have become the masters both politically and socially. Both the Chinese central government and all Chinese people as a whole have given their full support to the cause; today, the Tibetan people are becoming all the more united as they commit themselves to change, leaving behind the repression of the old and welcoming with open arms a land open to economic and cultural prosperity, social progress, a favorable ecological environment, and the most happiness ever seen on the faces of those living a good life on the Qinghai-Tibet plateau.

In the midst of such historic advancement, we welcome yet another occasion for celebration: the 30-year anniversary of the issue of *China's Tibet*.

The central government of the People's Republic of China has long been concerned with how best to introduce Tibet and its great achievements to the world. In 1989, *China's Tibet* was launched to do its part in attaining such a substantial feat. That year was a significant year: Tibet was facing turmoil at the hands of various foreign separatists who had their focus on Lhasa, and various rumors were incited among the people, leading them to call for "Tibet's independence". It was in such a rocking boat of an environment that *China's Tibet* took ink to paper as a form of public media focusing on providing people both at home and abroad an image of how things were really faring for the people of Tibet.

All staff, journalists, and even chief editors that ever had the opportunity to work for *China's Tibet* throughout the past three decades never failed to keep in mind the task at hand, regardless of the tide of the times. Equipped with a high level of dedication as well as political sensitivity, they have united not only those in Tibetan academia, but also those on Tibet's frontlines of development, regardless of their ethnicity or walk of life, all while honing in on their initiative, bringing out their fullest of enthusiasm to show both China and the rest of the world that the sun does shine upon the Qinghai-Tibet Plateau. *China's Tibet* has, since its foundation, become a garden for depicting a beautiful tomorrow, a window through which we can witness cutting-edge and extensive cultural exchanges, and a piece of land for the world to admire.The publication has been made available in three languages (Chinese, Tibetan, and English), and no matter which version, certain themes prevail, while there are some unique articles written for readers of one particular language to enjoy as a way to make each version have its own focus and individualized content. A massive amount of work goes into every single article, and by the time one finally makes its way onto the page, countless hours have been dedicated to its writing, organization, and editing, producing physical mementos of the great amount of responsibility and accountability journalists and editors bear to present readers a complete issue for their enjoyment. These articles are embodiments not only of deep exploration and reflection, but also of great attention and extreme focus to show Tibet's progress and advancement as well as the colorful lives of ethnic Tibetans, whose intricate culture has stood the test of time.

With it being 70 years since the founding of the People's Republic of China as well as 60 years since the onset of Tibet's unprecedented reform, *China's Tibet* has decided to launch its own celebratory program—30 Years of Fine Publications—bent toward recording Tibet's social and economic transformation as well as the colorful lives of those who call the world's most charming highland their home. This series of fine publications will be distributed in nine volumes, five in Chinese, respectively *Review the History of Tibet* (two volumes), *Scenery on the Roof of the World*, *People at the Snow-covered Land*, and *New Life on the Highland*; two in Tibetan, i.e., *Spring on the Highland* (two volumes); and two in English named *People on the Qinghai-Tibet Plateau* and *Life on the Qinghai-Tibet Plateau.*

In all reality, 30 years is not too long a time. Many things standing then are still standing today, but the people and their mindsets are by far not the same. That said, we can by no means be sure that we are able to extract the most precious of pearls among the great treasure trove of stories out there. What we can be sure of, however, is that every single individual editor of this journal has put great time, effort, and dedication to make sure that what was bound and distributed was absolutely the best they could do. How could we ever do such a task, though, without thinking of our gratitude to our previous leaders, those who first bore the torch of triumph as reporters and editors, those who passionately wrote, and those who enthusiastically awaited their next copies? Across the span of 30 years, our hearts go out in appreciation to all who contributed to our journal's success, and a most special thanks goes out to our great motherland, a nation that has granted a magnificent new era and made it possible for its people to stand in pride once again, full of strength and driven toward prosperity!

Socialism with Chinese characteristics has taken our country, lifted it on high, and marched it toward an era like never before. The Information Age has also done wonders to digitalize the entire world. In 2016, by following the trend of the times, the journal *China's Tibet* merged with *China Tibet Online* (tibet.cn) to start its new journey in pursuit of recording, writing down, and eulogizing the new era and to share stories of a more modern Tibet.

May blessings rain down upon our sweet motherland! May the sun of prosperity shine brightly upon Tibet!

Editorial Board of
30 Years of Fine Publications of China's Tibet
August 27, 2019

CONTENTS

1
THE BOYHOOD OF THE 10TH PANCHEN LAMA

Text by Yongzin Gyayag

The 10th Panchen Erdini Qoigyi Gyaincain was born in 1938, or, to be exact, the third day of the first month of the year of the Tiger in the 16th Tibetan calendrical cycle, in Beudu Township's Mari Village, Xunhua County, Qinghai Province. His father, Yabxi Gurgon Cedan, was a Dongbon, the township head. His mother's name was Yabxi Soinam Zholma. The Cedans bore the same family name as Pagba, the Sagya sect leader of the Tibetan Buddhism.

According to *Annals of Beudu Monastery*, when Aadan, a Sagya family member from Tibet, arrived at Beudu Township by way of Amdo and Rongwo counties, he met by chance a woodman out collecting firewood. Impressed by Aadan's handsome look and refined behavior, the woodman invited him to sit on a blanket of tree twigs for a chat. During the conversation, the man talked Aadan into settling down in Beudu Township, and soon, because of his wisdom, kindness and fair judgement, Aadan was made head of the township. Later, his seven sons each became the head of a tribe which made up the township's seven villages.

Beudu Township, located 15 kilometers to the southwest of the Xunhua County seat, lay astride three valleys, Zhongku, Mangyul and Xongyul, on the southern bank of the Yellow River. The local people were mostly peasants

Vice Chairman Zhu De (Left 3, front row) and Premier Zhou Enlai (Right 1, front row) welcome the Tenth Panchen Lama at Beijing Railway Station on Sep. 4, 1954.

and herdsmen, living off a warm climate and vast tracks of virgin forests and pastureland. All were pious Buddhists closely connected with such major religious establishments in Gansu and Qinghai as the Labrang, Tar Rongwo and Qakyunggon monasteries. Beudu Township itself boasted the famous Beudu Monastery, located on a slope south of the Mari Village, which, as legend has it, was built 500 years ago by Kanggar Gyacan, a famous monk of the Sagya sect. The monastery was later converted to the Gelug sect.

Propitious Sign

The morning of the day the boy who was to become the 10th Panchen was born, people of the Mari Village were burning mulberry trees on the slopes of the Riwoqe Hill behind the Dongbon's home as a sacrificial offering to the God. It snowed and a rainbow appeared. Struck by this strange phenomenon, villagers believed that the family of their leader would be fortunate. If his wife, who had been pregnant for sometime, should give birth today, they said, it would be a boy who could inherit his father's work. The night before, Aaku Gyalcan, the wife's brother, had a dream in which the Riwoqe Hill was enshrouded in yellow satin. Naturally, when the boy was born, everybody believed that he was special. The boy was named Gonbo Cedan.

Moving into Beudu Monastery

Gonbo Cedan frequently fell sick in the first three years of his life. No doctor could cure him, and during a particularly severe illness at the age of three, he was near death.

The township head was at his wit's end and asked Lakocang Jigme Chinlei Gyaco, a relative, for advice. Lakocang, a knowledgeable and prestigious lama at the Labrang Monastery and the scriptural tutor for the 9th Panchen, answered that Gonbo could get better only when he was sent to a lamasery to become a lama. The family and fellow villagers held a meeting and a consensus was reached that, since the boy was the only child of the Dongbon and since all signs had ordained that he would inherit his father's position, he could by no means become a lama. In order to treat his disease, however, he should be sent to live in a lamasery under the protection of the Buddha. As a result, three-year-old Gonbo was sent to reside in the Beudu Monastery, where, as a resident, he was not required to read Buddhist sutras or wear kasaya, a patchwork outer vestment worn by a Buddhist monk.

Child Prodigy

After he moved into the Beudu Monastery, Gonbo's sickness was quickly cured. During the three years in the monastery, he sometimes amused himself in the compound and sometimes listened to lamas as they recited the scriptures. Sometimes he was so homesick that he would flee to his family, only to be sent back time and again. He was known for his unusual talent, possibly hereditary, of being able to make and offer alms or make lucky knots with ropes at a very early age.

Many stories about his childhood are still familiar to monks in the monastery today. Once, at age four, talking to a lama in his family, he said he was soon to become a lama. Visiting the study of a Geshi, doctor of religion, he took one of the Buddhist writings from the bookshelves, and told his host that he would someday be able to recite it. The Geshi was surprised to find that the book the boy took was *Cema Namzhel*, a major Buddhist sutra all lamas of the Tashilhunpu Monastery were required to study. To be sure, the Geshi told himself, the boy was exceptionally talented.

Search for an Incarnate

The 9th Panchen, whose name was Chokyi Nyima, arrived at the Tar Monastery in 1935, or the fourth month of the Year of Wood Pig of the 16th Tibetan calendrical cycle, after a long journey from the interior of China. After staying there for almost a year, he left the Tar Monastery in the Year of the Fire Rat and when he stopped at the Labrang Monastery, he sent Living Buddha Zhudgu Rinpoche to the Tar Monastery to present 88 silver ingots and cook tea for the lamas as a gesture for the warm reception accorded him there. He finally arrived at the Gyegu Monastery in Yushu County, Qinghai, after a stop-over at the Dasi Jiala Monastery. Frustrated by his failure to return to Tibet because of obstruction by separatists in Lhasa, he died at the Gyegu Monastery in 1937, the Year of Fire Ox.

In 1941, the Year of Iron Snake, Losang Gyalcan, member of the Panchen field headquarters, arrived in Xining in search of the boy who was believe to be the reincarnation of the late 9th Panchen.

The Living Buddha Zhudgu Rinpoche of the Tashilhunpo Monastery was sent to Xunhua and Hualong for the purpose. Upon hearing that the Beudu Dongbon's son was especially talented, he visited the Tar Monerstery. After noting the names of the monastery and the boy, he returned to Shigatse without bothering to visit the boy's family.

A dozen children were picked in Qinghai and ten of them were chosen as candidates. The second year, when Gonbo Cedan was five, the Kampus Assembly (administration under the Panchen) took the ten to the Tar Monastery, where each of them was sent to live in a Garwa, the residence of a living Buddha. Gonbo Cedan stayed with me. Because the search for the incarnate was a top secret, at the time I did not know that something of great importance was happening. Gonbo left a few days later. I later learnt that the Abbot of the Tar Monastery had mingled the late Panchen's rosary and books with similar objects for the ten boys to pick through and choose. Gonbo picked up a finger ring used by the late Panchen, which earned him the first place among the ten boys.

Chosen as the New Panchen

After a series of screenings in 1943, only Gonbo, then six, and two other candidates were left. The Kampus Assembly again took them to the Tar Monastery, where, upon a decision of the monks, each candidate returned to the *garwa* where he had stayed a few years before. Thus, Gonbo stayed with me once again for seven months. At the time, the Kampus Assembly reported the progress of the work to the central KMT government and informed the Dalai Lama and his Gaxag government in Lhasa. A divination by the Dalai in the Jokhang Temple found Gonbo again on the top of the list.

The Gaxag government in Lhasa, while notifying the central KMT government of this result in a cable, suggested that the three boys be taken to Lhasa for a drawing of lots from a gold urn to decide the incarnate of the 9th Panchen. They declined, however, to invite a central government commissioner to supervise the drawing of lots and preside over the "sitting-in-bed" ceremony to swear in the new Panchen. This caused strong resentment on the part of the Kampus Assembly. Under these circumstances, the central KMT government withheld a decision regarding the matter.

The Panchen Kampus Assembly, then stationed in the residence of Living

Buddha Jamyang, after consultations with the Living Buddha Lakocang Jigme Chinlei Gyaco, decided that Gonbo Cedan was unquestionably the incarnate of the late Panchen. The reasons given were that, first, Gonbo came up first during the examination by the Kampus Assembly at the Tar Monastery and second, he was again on top of the list when the Dalai lama cast a divination at the Jokhang Temple. The last and most convincing evidence was that Buddhist experts observing the scenery of Lake Khamai Laco found that the images of building mirrored in the water were similar to that of the boy and that when the observation was drawing to an end they imagined a tiger followed by two rabbits in its wake. It happened that Gonbo was born in the Year of Tiger while the other two boys were born in the Year of Rabbit.

The lamas held that the KMT government was delaying its decision for too long, and, if the new Panchen was not installed at an early date, it would adversely affect his study of Buddhist scriptures. Thus, upon a joint decision made by the Kampus Assembly and Lakocang Gonbo Cedan was confirmed as the incarnate of the 9th Panchen.

Gonbo returned to Mari Village, Beudu Township, in the winter of 1943 to await his installments as the new Panchen. On the third day of the first month by Tibetan calendar, 1944, when he was only seven, the Kampus Assembly's representative came to take him away and, five days later, brought him to live again in my residence in the Tar Monastery. A "sitting-in-bed" ceremony to swear him in was held a week later by the Assembly at the monastery, or the Panchen's mansion. On the 15th day of the fourth month in the Tibetan calendar that year, the new Panchen was led to the Tar Monastery's golden hall and there he ascended to the seat placed in front of the silver pagoda of Zangkaba (Tsongkhapa), the esteemed spiritual leader of the Gelug sect.

The same day, ten Living Buddhas, headed by Lakocang and three Geshis, held a ceremony inaugurating the new Panchen's Buddhist life. At the ceremony, he was taught two Buddhist doctrines, *Genyan* and *Gecul*, had his hair cut by Lakocang, and was given the name Losang Chogyen Lhunzub Qoigyi Gyaincain.

In the fortnight that followed, Lakocang taught him part of the Buddhist classic *Gyuidesum* and related scriptures. The Kampus Assembly appointed Lakocang Jigme Gyaco and me as the 10th Panchen's scriptural tutors. I was also asked to look after his food, clothing, living, travel and sutra reading needs.

Learning Buddhist Canons

In 1945, when the 10th Panchen was eight, he finished a seven-month course given by Lakocang featuring such Buddhist classics as *Tuikor Doje Qoicog*. Contents of the course were decided by the Kampus Assembly.

In five years, from the age of 9 to 13, the Panchen finished his study of all the classics often read in the lamaseries. He also studied *Dode Kyanqen*, *Juijug*, *Qamqoi Denga* (including Parqin, *Dodekyan*, and *Gyui Lama*), *Cema Namzhel*, *Gyuidesum*, *Tuidor Qoiba* and *Jigqei Doje Wanggur*. He had mastered all the literature concerning Buddhist rituals and ceremonies.

"Sitting-in-Bed" Ceremony

In 1949 the Panchen turned 12. Qinghai Living Buddhas Serche, Tugan, Tuikor, Qoisang, Serdog, Minyag and Xeirab Gyaco as well as Mongolian and Tibetan nobilities signed a cable addressed to the KMT's Commission for Mongolian and Tibetan Affairs, demanding that the KMT government formerly endorse the new-found incarnate of the 9th Panchen and that the boy be escorted to the Tar Monastery for the "sitting-in-bed" ceremony, a function performed for the installation of the 7th Panchen Tenpai Nyima.

On June 2 that year, Acting President Li Zongren of the KMT government issued an order, approving Gonbo Cedan as the 10th Panchen Erdini without going through the formalities of "drawing lots from the gold urn." On August 10, 1949, or the third day of the seventh month of the Tibetan calendar, a solemn "sitting-in-bed" ceremony was held at the Jamwang Lhakang Hall of the Tar Monastery. It was presided over by Guan Jiyu, minister of the Commission for Mongolian and Tibetan Affairs, who read the approval granted by Li Zongren to the 10th Panchen, issued him a gold seal and presented him with gifts. Giris were also given to Living Buddha

Xabzhanggar (Abbot of the Tar Monastery) and the Mongolian and Tibetan Living Buddhas and nobilities who attended the function, as well as all the lamas of the Tar Monastery. Guan also issued alms to all the lamas of the monastery. The KMT official left on the sixth day of the seventh month, or August 13, 1949, a day before the Panchen and his entourage left the Tar Monastery for Xiangride.

Trip to Beijing

When the city of Xining was liberated on September 5, 1949, the People's Liberation Army immediately established contact with the Panchen, who was then living in Xiangride. When the People's Republic of China was founded on October 1 of that year, the Panchen, through his Kampus Assembly headquartered in the Tar Monastery, telegraphed Chairman Mao and Commander-in-Chief Zhu De, expressing his support for the Central People's Government. In July 1950, the Panchen returned to the Tar Monastery.

In April 1951, negotiations for the peaceful liberation of Tibet were begun in Beijing between a Central Government delegation and representatives of the Tibet local government. Panchen, invited by the Central Government as a special guest for the consultations, arrived in Beijing in late April that year with 40-odd religious and secular officials of the Kampus Assembly. I was one of the participating members of the delegation.

On May 24, the Kampus Assembly delegation paid tribute to Chairman Mao. The Panchen personally held a *khada* (a piece of silk as a greeting gift) in his hands and was followed by his father, Jijigme and Lhamon.

I was at the end of the procession holding a silk banner inscribed with the words, "To Chairman Mao, the great liberator of the Chinese people of all nationalities." The gifts also included the Buddhist statues, manzhu and boi (Tibetan incense).

After the ceremony, Li Weihan, head of the United Front Work Department of the Central Party Committee, had a five-minute chat with the Panchen, Jijigmei and me in Chairman Mao's bedroom. The chairman then threw a banquet in the Panchen's honor, attended by Commander-in-Chief Zhu De, Liu Shaoqi, Zhou Enlai and Deng Xiaoping. During the banquet, the Chairman inquired about the Kampus Assembly and had a cordial conversation with the Panchen. Afterwards, the Panchen left Beijing for a tour of Tianjin, Shanghai and Hangzhou before returning to the Tar Monastery at the end of the fifth month of the Tibetan calendar.

Entering Tibet

In the eighth month of that year, the Panchen finished reading the sutra *Tuikou Doje Qoicong* at the Tar Monastery visited the Labrang Monastery and returned to his hometown in Beudu Township. Asked to prepare for his entry into Tibet, he then returned to the Tar Monastery. On the 16th of the 12th month that year, the Panchen began his journey to Tibet. I was one of his entourage. Arriving in Lhasa in April 1952, he met with the Dalai Lama at the Potala Palace. On April 15, a "sitting-in-bed" ceremony was held in the Simqung Yigai Hall of the Tashilhunpo Monastery, and for the first time in his life, the Panchen ascended to the seat which the monastery had kept exclusively for all his predecessors.

In June that year, I transferred my position as scriptural tutor over to Geshi Gagen Nyima of the Tashilhunpo Monastery as I had decided, with the Panchen's approval, to Qinghai at the end of the year. During the New Year celebrations of 1953, lamas of the monastery asked that the major prayer ceremony Tuikor Doje Qoicong, which they had missed for so many years because of the absence of the Panchen, be held in March now that he was back. Acting on a request of the Kampus Assembly, I postponed my trip until after the ceremony.

I arrived in Nagqu County in May. There, I saw the Panchen, who was on his way to Bejjing for the First National People's Congress.

Issue: Spring, 1990.

2

JAMYANG BALMO: THE LAST DEGE HEADWOMAN

Text by Jiang Mingxue

Jamyang Balmo is a legendary figure about whose life there has been no detailed literary record. Asked by the Editorial Board of *China's Tibet*, the writer spoke with some people familiar with the late headwoman and took down their fragmentary but precious description of the last Dege Headwoman.

The Apple of Nangqen Headman's Eye

On November 25, 1913, a female baby was born into the family of the Headman of Nangqen in Qinghai Province, by the Zaqu River, at the upper reaches of the Lancang River.

In a traditional Tibetan family centered around males, the birth of this baby named Jamyang Balmo certainly brought no joy to the Headman. However, relatives and neighbors still took part in the celebration; religious activities were still held, the serfs continued their corvee labor and valuable objects were offered as gifts, The Headman himself came to regard the daughter as the apple of this eye.

As soon as Jamyang Balmo learned to speak, she began to receive an education in Tibetan history and culture. The education and the favorable influence of local People helped make Jamyang Balmo into an intelligent Tibetan girl.

Marriage with the Dege Headman

The water of the Zaqu River flowed unnoticed for another 24 years, at which time Jamyang Balmo was found one day by its bank, wearing her hair in many stringlike braids, decorated with beautiful ornaments at their ends, a symbol of her having reached maturity. Waving farewell to all she knew best, the horses and deers, the grassland stretching north to the Tangla Mountains, Jamyang Balmo took a tearful leave of her hometown and her parents. She had become the bride of Cewang Tondan, the 50th Dege Headman.

The wedding ceremony, luxurious and magnificent, reflected the strict marriage customs within the ruling class as the bridegroom attempted to restore the power and prestige of the Dege Headman through the marriage. This was necessary because Dege was of strategic importance in west Sichuan Province.

According to *Brief History of Dege Headmen of Various Generations*, authored by a Dege Headman Cewang Doje Rinzin, the first Dege Headman was during the Tang Dynasty (618–907). By the time of the 32nd Dege Headman, religious influence and marital ties had created a political and economic power base for the Dege. Between the Ming Dynasty (1368–1644) and the beginning of the Qing Dynasty (1644–1911), the Dege Headmen, backed by the central authorities, became overlord of the northern part of the former Xikang Province. The Dege's land at the time extended to both sides of the Jinsha River, including the five counties of Dege, Baiyu, Jiangda, Dankug and Serxu and part of Garze County in Sichuan Province and part of Madoi County of Qinghai Province, being then called Dege Gyalkab (Dege Kingdom).

Since the 44th Dege Headman, between the end of the Qing Dynasty and the beginning of the Republic of China (1912–1949), internal divisions appeared and the ensuing struggles for power caused the Dege Headman's power and influence to wane. When Cewang Tondan ascended the throne, the Dege Headman had only four counties under his rule: Dege, Baiyu, Serxu and Dankug. In order to prevent the clan's tragic downfall from engulfing him, the ambitious Cewang Tondan adopted the policy of building support through marriage relations, the same strategy which had once brought the former Dege such strength and power. His goal was to solidify his sphere of influence.

The Crisis of Headman's Successor

Three years later, in 1940, Cewang Tondan, discontent and regretful, died from an illness and left behind Jamyang Balmo and their only son, two-year-old Puga. According to the hereditary line of succession of the Dege Headman, the first son should become the abbot of Gonqen Monastery, the family temple, while the second son should inherit the Head man post as the head of the family. Other sons, if any, should practise Buddhism with their eldest brother in either the family temple or in other monasteries. If there was only one son, tradition held he should be in charge of the family temple and serve as a Headman, thus integrating politics with religion. The two-year-old Puga was, of course, too young to handle any affair and, so centering around the issue of who should succeed as Headman, fierce internal fight for power began.

Leaders from five main monasteries under the Dege Headman and all headmen representatives held meetings to discuss the issue. One opinion put forth was that the young Puga should succeed as Headman but that, temporarily, his mother Jamyang Balmo should act as regent. The group proposing this said that in the 39th year under the reign of Emperor Qianlong, Zhaxi Wangmo, wife of the 43rd Headman Lozhoi Gyaco, acted as regent after her husband's death because their son was too young.

Another group thought Jamyang Balmo should assume all the power of Headman for herself. They bolstered their proposal by saying that Nor Gyalbo had been in power for eight years before her son, the 45th Headman

Jamyang Balmo

Cewang Doje Rinzin, reached the age of 13. But those of the opposite opinion said that women were too short-sighted to have total control. When Nor Gyalbo was in power, they argued, she listened too much to the monks which in the end caused a rebellion by secular headmen.

Facing with so many factions each trying to cheat and outwit the other, Jamyang Balmo nearly returned to her parents' home with her son.

The 51st Dege Headwoman

What made this 27-year-old woman plunge into the perilous whirlpool of feudal politics and, in the end, the power of Headman?

As each faction held its ground, Jamyang Balmo, in a confused and contradictary state of mind, visited Gonqen Monastery, a stronghold of the Sagya Sect. The 700-year-old monastery was built by Lozhoi Dobdan, the 33rd Dege Headman, to commemorate his ancestors' virtuous conduct in worshipping the head of Sagya sect. As time passed, it gradually became the centre of power of the Dege Headman and was formally named "Dege", meaning "auspicious land". In the monastery's Scripture Hall, unique and lively frescos displayed the prosperous history of the Dege headman in bright yet solemn decoration.

"Seeing them," Jamyang Balmo recalled many years later, "one couldn't help trembling with excitement and marveling at our ancesters' heroic undertakings."

She then went to the famous Dege Scripture Printing Hall and as she looked up to the top terrace at the gold wheel and peacock bestowed by the Qing Emperor Yongzheng, tears dropped from her eyes. She understood well that Dege, as in the saying "Heaven Dege and Earth Dege," symbolized the prestigious position and power of the Dege Headman. All depended, however, on the approval and generosity of the central government, Jamyang Balmo felt a sense of mission, a sense that she could no longer escape a historical choice. She decided to take upon herself the title of 51st Dege Headman. Thereafter, she pushed herself squarely onto the stage of feudal politics, a political arena mixed in crisis because of local divisions.

Failure of Ten-year Effort

It took great effort for her to carry on her work under such difficult circumstances. She was not only obliged to act as a Headwoman and thus carry out all duties which fell under the Dege Headman's Jurisdiction, but also to fulfil her role as a mother. Remembering the lesson of Nor Gyalbo, she concentrated all real power in her own hands and delegated matters of little consequence to lower levels. Gradually, she won people's respect.

The frequent internal conflicts, however, continued. Xabgab Dobdan, a powerful headman, organized an opposition and openly proposed that he should be the prince regent. This led to fights. Jamyang Balmo later said that the ten years of holding onto power nearly killed her.

After Liberation—A New Situation

In October 1949, immediately after receiving the news that her hometown Nangqen was liberated, Jamyang Balmo sent her trusted manager Oma Xianzi to go to the PLA troops at Yushu, to express her support for the liberation forces.

In spring 1950, Jamyang Balmo asked Xabgab Dobdan to go to Chongqing to meet Liu Bocheng and Deng Xiaoping and invite the People's Liberation Army to enter Xikang and to liberate Tibet. When the People's Liberation Army did enter Xikang, Jamyang Balmo sent Big Headman Puchugchug to meet them at Kangding in her name.

"At that time, I seemed to be enlightened and guided by Buddha," Jamyang Balmo recalled.

The liberation of Xikang not only saved the Tibetan people from misery but also extricated Jamyang Balmo from her predicament. She knew that the rumors created by the KMT reactionaries and a handful of separatists, taking advantage of her disagreement with Xabgab Dobdan, had fostered a feeling of insecurity and instability in the area. It was the Party and the Central Government that mediated the disagreement between them and effectively prevented the civil strife which had so often occured in Dege's history. Her biggest concern was dispelled.

In November 1950, Jamyang Balmo took the post of vicechairman of the Chamdo Liberation Committee and later became a member of the Xikang provincial people's government; Xabgab Dobdan and Puchugchug also assumed posts in the government. "If there had been no Communist Party," said Jamyang Balmo, "I would have been swallowed up by either feudal factionalism or the KMT reactionaries. Without the Communist Party, I would not have become what I am today."

Assisting the PLA's Entrance Into Tibet

Using her position and popular support, Jamyang Balmo actively assisted the PLA troops'entrance into Tibet. On the eve of Chamdo's liberation,

Jamyang Balmo sent Oma Xianzi to persuade Dege Galsang Wangdui, a relative of the Dege Headman and the Dapon (regimental commander) of the Ninth Regiment of Tibetan Army, to support the PLA. Meanwhile, co-operating with her former "adversary" Xabgab Dobdan, she motivated the masses to organize a transport corps of 10,000 yaks. Struggling from Mani Kanggar to Chamdo through the harsh climate, the corps provided foodstuffs and equipment to the liberation army who were building the Xikang-Tibet Highway as they entered Tibet.

General Chen Mingyi, commander and political commissar of the rear troops of PLA's 18th Corps, said Jamyang Balmo played an important role in the peaceful liberation of Tibet. If she had not organized the masses to support the front line and insured the area's social stability, the PLA's progress would have been affected.

Attending the National Day Celebration

In 1952, the Xikang Tibet Autonomous Region arranged for a delegation to participate in the National Day celebration in Beijing. Acting as deputy head of the delegation, Jamyang Balmo, representing all Tibetan compatriots in Xikang area, presented a *khada* to Chairman Mao Zedong of the Central People's Government. In return, Chairman Mao gave gifts to all the representatives, including Jamyang Balmo who received a brocade Tibetan robe. Treasuring it as a special honor, Jamyang Balmo was reluctant to wear it for years.

At that time, the Tibetan delegation sent by the 10th Panchen Lama was also in Beijing for National Day celebration. When meeting the two delegations, Mao said that social reform in the Tibetan regions was an important point of the 17-Article Agreement for the peaceful liberation of Tibet. It conformed with basic interests of the millions of serfs and was of benefit not only for the development of Tibetan regions, but for national unity as well. The timing of reform, Mao added, depended on developments in Tibetan regions and consultation with both the upper social strata and the masses. Chairman Mao sincerely and earnestly urged them to stand with the masses and be of one heart and mind with the central authorities, to transform their society and to take the broad road of socialism. Jamyang Balmo later recalled that Chairman Mao's words gave her a greater understanding of the Communist Party of China's policy towards nationalities.

Assisting the Government in Democratic Reform

At the end of 1955, according to the policy of peaceful consultation, Sichuan's Tibetan areas began democratic reform. The key task was agrarian reform, specifically the confiscation of the serfowners' and the landowners' surplus land for distribution to poor peasants with no or little land. It was to be a major step in the abolition of feudal privilege and exploitation and the complete liberation of serfs and other working people.

Jamyang Balmo had mentally prepared herself for the day. After cadres from the superior authorities explained to her the general and specific policies of the democratic reform, she took the lead in handing over her surplus land and private arms. Moreover, she set the serfs free and sold the grains the Dege family had accumulated over years to the state.

Of course, the democratic reform was not a quick and easy process for Jamyang Balmo. She was born into a feudal family and had enjoyed the privileges of Headman and so felt somewhat reluctant to part with them. At first, indeed, she had some very confused ideas.

A Talk with Zhou Enlai

In December 1956, Jamyang Balmo was invited to attend the Second Session of the First National People's Congress (NPC). During this session, Premier Zhou Enlai told her that the democratic reform was aimed at changing the backward feudal production relations in the Tibetan areas, the emancipation of the productive forces, and enabling the broad masses of Tibetan people to truly enjoy equality and just rights. A patriot, he told her, should trust the Party's policy and serve as a link to assist the local government in accomplishing the democratic reform. His words cleared up misunderstanding Jamyang Balmo had and reinforced her confidence to follow the Communist Party and the socialist road.

Never Sadden the Beloved, Never Gladden the Foe

Back from Beijing and taking advantage of her influence, Jamyang Balmo went to areas of rebellion to persuade those who had been hoodwinked to oppose the central authorities. She reasoned with them that since the founding of the people's government, the Xikang-Tibet and Qinghai-Tibet highways across the "roof of the world" and a bridge over the Jinsha River had been built. As a result, it was more convenient for their pilgramage to Lhasa; large quantities of materials for production and daily life could also be transported to benefit Tibet's development. Moreover, she argued, many PLA soldiers had given their lives to the cause. Although the KMT government had also announced plans to build the Xikang-Qinghai Highway, not an inch had been constructed except by forced donation, abuse of labor and corruption. It proved, she said, that the Communist Party was sincere in its help and assistance and that it wanted the Tibetan people to have equal position and rights. How could one, she asked, requite kindness with enmity, saddening the beloved but gladdening the foe?

From Headwoman to Citizen

After democratic reform in Sichuan's Tibetan areas was accomplished, the feudal serf system was abolished and more than 20,000 slaves liberated from serfdom. The Dege Headman system, which had begun with Londongtsan, a minister of Songtsen Gambo during the Tubo Kingdom, finally stepped down from the stage of history after 51 generations, nearly 1,000 years. Jamyang Balmo said emotionally that although her life as Headwoman had ended, she would start a brandnew life as a citizen in New China. This was worth her lifetime pursuit and struggle, she said.

It was the same lofty beliefs that had kept her undismayed during the chaotic "cultural revolution" (1966–76), and gave her the wherewithal to withstand the most difficult and trying circumstances.

Serve the People as Much as Possible

In 1978, Jamyang Balmo was again elected deputy to the NPC, member of the NPC's Nationalities Commission, and vice-chairman of the Sichuan Provincial Political Consultative Conference. Her beloved son, Puga, was a member of the Standing Committee of the Garze Tibet Autonomous Prefecture. Considering her age and her physical condition at the time, the government helped to move her family to Chengdu, capital of Sichuan Province.

Jamyang Balmo said, "I am most grateful to the Party's policy. But what I've done is far from enough. I shall work for the people as much as possible for the rest of my life."

When she learned that a few separatists had begun riots in Lhasa, Jamyang Balmo was indignant and said. "Tibet is all inseparable part of the motherland since ancient times. Any words and deeds attempting to split the motherland is a mistake and against the basic interests of the broad masses. It will inevitably be resisted and cast aside by the Tibetan people."

She wrote letters to overseas Tibetan compatriots, relatives and friends to dispel their misgivings. One letter reads: By comparing the old and new society, I see clearly that only after the founding of New China, under the leadership of the Communist Party of China, did we Tibetans completely abolish the system of national oppression and smash the yoke holding down the Tibetan people. The Communist Party of China is indeed a political party which extricates all nationalities from misery and works for the interests of all the people.

In September 1988, Jamyang Balmo died of illness in Chengdu at the age of 75. Compared with Zhaxi Wangmo and Nor Gyalbo, two previous Dege Headwomen, she was fortunate. She kept pace with the times; she had upheld patriotism, unity and progress all her life. For this, she deserves the respect and commemoration of all people.

Issue: Spring, 1990.

3
FROM GESHI OF SERA MONASTERY TO KMT ATTACHE

Text by Xerab Nyima

The deafening sound of drums and musical instruments resounded in Gyaincain—Official Greeting Pavilion—in the western suburb of Lhasa on February 16, 1930 as Tibetan government officials stood seriously in line waiting for someone to arrive.

"Who is he?" asked onlookers with great interest.

When he finally came, they were astonished to find an ordinary abbot called Goinqog Zongnyi from the Sera Monastery.

A Geshi

Goinqog Zongnyi was born into an honest family in Lhasa in 1883. At nine, he was tonsured in Sera, one of the three most important monasteries in Lhasa. He was charged with striking the morning bell and doing odd work but spent more time studying the Tibetan language and Buddhist scriptures.

The young monk was so clever that he could recite numerous sutras, enjoying some fame in the monastery for his abilities. At 20, he won the Geshi (first-class Buddhist doctorate) degree.

It was around this time that the 13th Dalai Lama began to see the true nature of the British imperialists and decided to strengthen ties with the

Yonghegong Lamasery in Beijing, where Goinqog Zongnyi once served as an abbot.

Central Government. He looked for an abbot from either of the three major monasteries, to whom he might entrust this task.

In Beijing

The 13th Dalai Lama picked Goinqog Zongnyi because even though he was only a young monk he was also wise.

In August 1923, the Dalai Lama officially ordered Goinqog Zongnyi to travel to Beijing to take up the post as the abbot of the Yonghegong Lamasery.

Goinqog Zongnyi left Lhasa for Beijing together with 10 of his disciples immediately after receiving the appointment, arriving on January 23, 1924.

As the Dalai Lama had appointed Goinqog personally, the KMT government accepted him even though tradition demanded that the man the Dalai Lama dispatched should serve as the abbot of the Yonghegong Lamasery.

In the early winter of 1924, General Feng Yuxiang led his troops into

Beijing, where they camped in the Palace Museum much to the suspicion of the Mongolians and Tibetans.

Goinqog Zongnyi Joined other Tibetan abbots in Beijing in asking the KMT government whether Central Government policy had changed towards Tibet. Four days later the KMT government said there would be no change in the treatment of either the Manchus, Mongolians, Hui or Tibetan peoples.

In August 1925, Goinqog Zongnyi, as the representative of Tibet,was employed as a member of the "constitution drafting committee," working on the constitution for China.

When Chiang Kai-shek as the commander-in-chief of the national revolutionary army, paid a visit to Beijing in August 1928, he met with Goinqog Zongnyi who expressed his views on the settlement of the Tibetan issue, leaving a deep impression on Chiang.

KMT Attache

In June 1929, Goinqog Zongnyi was invited to attend a ceremony held specially for Sun Yatsen in Nanjing but an illness prevented him from accepting.

Two months later, he went to Taiyuan, where he was met by Yan Xishan, the head of the Mongolian-Tibetan Committee. He told Yan that the Dalai Lama had no intention of forming an alliance with the British and held no hatred for the Han. He also passed on the good wishes of the Dalai Lama for the return of Panchen Erdeni to Tibet.

On September 3, he went to Nanjing where he was met by Chiang Kai-shek. He told Chiang "Tibet will be obedient to the Central Government absolutely. The first step is for Tibet to resume the ties it had forged with the Central Government in the past."

As a result of Goinqog Zongnyi's comments, the Central Government gained a better understanding of the Tibetan issue, and decided to send an official into Tibet for consultation with the Dalai Lama or invite a representative of the Dalai Lama or invite a representative of the Dalai Lama to Nanjing. As a token of sincerity and friendliness, the Central Government decided to send Goinqog Zongnyi into Tibet as its special attache.

In December 1929, Goinqog Zongnyi went to Tibet, taking his letter of appointment detailing his special position, Chiang Kai-shek's letter to the Dalai Lama, a photo of Chiang, a cipher book from the Central Government, the eightarticle document of the Mongolian-Tibetan Committee on the solution of the Tibetan issue, Chiang's letter to Carong Dasang Zhamdong, and Yan Xishan's letter to the Dalai Lama.

Chiang told the Dalai Lama in his letter that he would send an official into Tibet for contact with the Dalai Lama or the Dalai Lama could send his representative to Nanjing for contact with the Central Government.

In other words, Goinqog Zongnyi was essentially that very Central Government official, instead of merely being the abbot Stationed in Beijing by the three major monasteries of Lhasa. This is why the Dalai Lama gave Goinqog Zongnyi a red-carpet welcome when he reached Lhasa.

Highest Treatment

When Goinqog Zongnyi reached Lhasa, he sent a cable to the Central Government, saying that he had received special treatment, that the Tibetans were very glad to see an attache of the Central Government and that the Tibetan issue would certainly be settled at an early date.

Later, when he reported to the Central Government, Goinqog Zongnyi said, "The Dalai Lama was far-sighted and had maintained political ties with the Central Government in the 10 years of seclusion. When I returned to Lhasa upon orders of the Central Government, all Tibetan officials came to greet me at the Norbu Lingka (the Summer Palace of the Dalai Lama), where the Dalai lama rose to his feet to receive all documents from the Central Government as a token of his respect. "

Dalai's Delegate

In March 1930, the Dalai Lama sent Goinqog Zongnyi to Nanjing as his chief representative charged with handling Tibet's ties with the Central Government and making preparations for the establishment of a Tibet Office in Nanjing.

After setting up the Tibet Office, Goinqog Zongnyi worked very hard and in May of the same year served as one of the five representatives of the Dalai Lama to attend a "national assembly" of the Central Government.

On September 18, when the Japanese invaded Shenyang in northeast China, Goinqog Zongnyi took an active part in the organization of the "Xikang-Tibetan compatriots association for national salvation."

At the head of the Tibet Office, he joined an anti-Japanese parade organized by Xikang-Tibetan compatriots in Nanjing. During this period of time, he and his Tibet Office members joined the KMT Party, and he attended the fourth KMT national congress on November 12.

Later, he attended the fifth KMT national congress. Tibet's ties with the Central Government were thus normalized, and the Central Government commended Goinqog Zongnyi for his contribution in this matter.

On December 17, 1933, the 13th Dalai Lama passed away and Goinqog Zongnyi reported the news to the Central Government. He cooperated with members of the Tibet Office in writing *The Dalai Lama*, in which he referred most positively to the life of the Dalai Lama, especially his efforts toward establishing the normalization of relations with Central Government.

Thanks to Goinqog Zongnyi's efforts, Huang Musong, a Central Government official, went to Tibet to attend the funeral ceremony for the late Dalai Lama, the first time a Central Government official had visited Tibet since the 1911 Revolution, which toppled the Qing Dynasty (1644–1911).

In April 1934, Goinqog Zongnyi applied for retirement, and the Tibetan government approved his application. After returning to Tibet he died of illness on March 8, 1944 at the age of 61.

Issue: No.1, 1995.

4

A MAN DIES FOR TIBETANS

Text by Yeixi Gyaco

The first half of the last decade of this century drew to a close with a common topic of conversation amongst Tibetans centering on a man of the Han nationality. Elderly Tibetans said he was better than their own children, while children addressed him as Uncle Kong. The people's government of Tibet Autonomous Region referred to him as "an outstanding member of the Communist Party of China, an exemplary representative of Han cadre sent to assist the Tibetans, a man who contributed to national unity, a model for leading cadres to emulate, and a public servant of the Tibetans."

He was none other than my dear friend Kong Fansen, a man I considered as the most outstanding Han cadre in Tibet. "Elderly Tibetans are my folks, and children in Tibet are the same as mine," Kong often said, adding, "Tibet is my second home."

Govn't Call

Kong Fansen was born into a poor peasant family in Wulidun Village, Liaocheng City, Shandong Province. In 1979, at the age of 34, he answered the Central Government call to "assist with Tibet's economic development and help improve the lives of Tibetans." Kong journeyed to Tibet despite the fact that his mother was approaching 80, and that his wife was physically weak and prone to illness. What's more, he had three children, the eldest of whom was only eight years old. When asked whether or not he would go, Kong responded: "Tibet needs Han cadres to assist in economic development. I am always prepared to go so long as I fulfill the requirements. I will obey the decision of the Party organization and will go no matter the difficulties with which I'm confronted."

The journey to Tibet was far from uneventful, with the bus breaking down in the Tanggula Mountains. The passengers were forced to spend the night in the thin air of the mountains. On this particular night he experienced difficult life on the Qinghai-Tibet Plateau for the first time, and gained a deeper understanding of the true value of the aid Tibet program.

Kong Fansen was assigned to work as the deputy Party secretary of Kamba County in Shigatse. Life in Kamba, which sits at an elevation of 4,578 meters above sea level, was far from easy, a fact often compounded by the severe weather characteristic of its location high in the mountains in the western part of this wonderland of snow.

Kong threw himself into his work from the very beginning, despite the fact that he experienced great difficulty recovering from dizziness. He frequently rode long distances by horseback to visit the remote homes of herdsmen and farmers, living and working with them for various periods to gain greater insight into their lifestyles and needs.

Kong managed to establish deep friendships with the Tibetans in a short span of only three years, with each and every one speaking highly of his work. He completed his assignment and returned home in early 1982.

Tibet Revisited

Kong returned to Tibet in 1988. His accomplishments during the first visit to Tibet proved him to be a good man and model cadre, facts which did not go unnoticed by the Shandong provincial government. It decided that he should return.

By that time, Kong had been promoted a high-level position as deputy

Kong Fansen (Right) visits Yeshe Drolma, an elderly widow, in the Ritu County of Ngari.

head of Liaocheng Prefecture. The situation was further complicated by the fact that his mother was approaching 90, his wife was sick and his children were attending school. Kong hesitated in the face of seemingly insurmountable difficulties.

In the end, however, the determined Kong announced his decision. Eyes filled with filial tears, Kong told his elderly mother: "Mom, I'm going to attend a meeting in a faraway place. Please take care."

Just prior to departing for Tibet, Kong fell on his knees kowtowing to his mother, not knowing whether he would see her again as she reached the twilight of her life.

This time around, Kong Fansen was assigned to a position as the deputy mayor of Lhasa. Immediately after reporting to the city government, Kong approached Mayor Lobgar, a Tibetan, requesting a work assignment, and was placed in charge of education and civil affairs. Within a short period of only 20 days, Kong visited seven counties under the jurisdiction of Lhasa.

On one particular day, during a visit to a village school in Karub Township, Nyemo County, Kong was quite surprised to find one teacher and only six students. Thoughts of the school's poverty remained constantly on his mind. In the summer of 1990, he returned to the county on a fact-finding mission, and while there provided assistance necessary to move the school to a better location.

Staying Put

Kong Fansen was originally scheduled to return to Shandong Province in early 1993 upon completion of his mission in Tibet. However, he agreed to repeated requests that he stay. During his prolonged tenure, Kong was assigned to a position as Party secretary of the Ngari Prefecture, one of the poorest areas in Tibet.

Since Ngari was my hometown, I have a clear understanding of the economic situation at that time. The prefecture was in sore need of the care and support of the Central Government and people from the hinterland. Kong approached the difficult situation with an iron-clad mind.

Orphans

Tibetans continue to talk fondly about the fact that Kong adopted two Tibetan orphans during his stay in the region.

In the summer of 1992, a devastating earthquake hit Yangrigang Township, Maizhokunggar County, Lhasa City. Kong, vice-mayor of Lhasa at the time, discovered that three Tibetan children—Gongsang, Quying and Qunyian—had lost their parents and homes during the disaster. Kong adopted the three children despite the already heavy burden of his family and low salary. Lobsang Toinzhub, vice-chairman of the people's government of Tibet Autonomous Region, relieved at least a portion of Kong's burden by adopting Qunyian.

Kong exhibited his great affection for Gongsang and Quying, who in turn addressed his as "grandpa." Kong's first concern after work was to cook meals for the children. Kong would immediately seek medical attention if either child fell ill. He also ensured the children had adequate clothing. Kong later contributed 200 yuan each month to house the children at the Maizhokunggar Primary School. Kong's care and concern seemed endless.

The two boys later transferred to the Gar Primary School in Shiquanhe Town, Ngari, with the dedicated Kong cycling a long distance to ensure they had adequate food and meat. Each weekend, Kong provided generous entertainment for the children in his home.

In 1993, Kong sold 900 mm of blood to a local hospital to ensure the children had adequate support. The Gar Primary School sponsored a sports meet in late May 1994. Obliging as ever, Kong paid 11,050 yuan to outfit 103 children with new sports shoes.

"We dearly love these shoes and are afraid they will be damaged if we wear them," said a student by the name of Cebai Doje. "In fact, we wear them only on holidays and during sports meet."

Kong's sincerity has moved even ballad singers. "I've been singing the praises of heroes for my entire life," said Puncong Lhunzhub, a performer famous for his portrayal of King Gesar, "I think Kong is a true hero."

"I have five children, Kong visted our village providing us with medicine and offering to support one of my children."

Although over 20 years of age, Kong's eldest son had spent only five years with his father. His daughters had spent even less time with their father. Kong was strict with his children.

In a letter to his daughter Kong Ling, he wrote: "Dear Ling, I have been very busy and have not written for a long period. I am glad to learn that you are very active in school. This represents quite a change from when you

parents. It's obvious that you are now mature. One must do things for oneself. Don't you agree?"

Loving Caring

Kong has visited 48 of Lhasa's 55 nursing homes. In the winter of 1990, during a fact-finding mission to review educational work in Doilungdeqen County, Lhasa, Kong braved heavy snow and bone chilling winds to visit the Sangda Township Nursing Home. He not only delivered a package of medicine, but also reviewed the living conditions of the patients and offered to provide them with physical examinations.

Upon finding that one elderly woman known as Grandma Qungzong was wearing a pair of tattered shoes, he immediately grasped her swollen feet and attempted to warm them with his own body heat. Tears rolled down the cheeks of Qungzong, a deaf-mute, as she watched this previously unknown man of the Han nationality treat her with such kindness.

Kong later returned to Lhasa and immediately sent a pair of new cotton padded shoes to the unfortunate elderly woman. Qungzong took great pains with the shoes, going so far as to place them by her pillow as she slept. Qungzong wrote, "I could not fall asleep unless I knew the shoes were safe."

Kong's mind was constantly filled with thoughts of elderly Tibetans, especially those without a family. In June 1993, while leading a fact-finding mission to Burang County, Kong happened on two Gar County widows, one in her 70s and the other her 90s. He offered suggestions to help them lead a better life, and before departing offered to give them his own money. Thereafter, other people sent daily necessities to the two elderly Tibetan women.

On the first day of the first Tibetan month in 1994, Kong joined with other leaders of the Lhasa government on a visit to veteran government functionaries in Ngari. Kong visited 40-odd households on the very first day. One individual named Benqung recalled, "Kong visited to inquire about my health and living conditions. He advised me to enter some type of business after retirement."

Shortly after retiring, Benqung purchased highland barley to brew wine. She earned close to 1,000 yuan from the venture in the first six months. According to Kong, "Elderly government functionaries have dedicated their life to work for a better Ngari. We should show great concern for them and enable them to happily enjoy the twilight of their life."

Soon after this visit, the area received much needed facilities, including a clinic, a dining hall and recreation center. Acting on the advice of Kong, four elderly men opened a teahouse.

Kong spent the Tibetan New Year in Ngari, unable to find time to join his elderly mother and family in Shandong.

Public Service

No matter where, Kong Fansen remained a dedicated public servant, regardless of whether in Kamba County, Lhasa, Ngari or any other location on the Roof of the World.

Kong fainted and fell from his horse during one particular visit to Kamba County. Local Tibetans rushed him to a hospital some 15 km away.

"Tibetans are very good to me," said Kong after regaining consciousness. Thereafter, Kong developed an enduring friendship with the Kamba people. In fact, he visited each and every household in Canglung Township, the poorest area in the county. In the fall of 1989, Kong returned to Canglung in his capacity as the vice-mayor of Lhasa City. Kong's mother was at her home in Shandong celebrating her 90th birthday. Warm tears streamed down Kong's cheeks as he knelt in the direction of Shandong to kowtow to his mother. He then went to a local post office with the full intention of sending his mother some money. Kong opened his wallet and checked his limited fund. He then realized that he was about to visit the poor people of Canglung, and with a heavy heart decided against sending money to this mother.

The people of Canglung were delighted to see Kong. They threw a party in the home of Gerab, with entertainment and treats such as moon cakes and fruit provided by Kong...

Bold Decision

While in Ngari, Kong visited 98 of 106 townships in only one year. In 1992, Ngari was hit by a drought followed by a heavy snowstorm which together threatened the existence of the local people. The drought in fact killed large numbers of livestock and river channels were dry.

Kong stayed with the locals for months on end to search for a solution. Based on a thorough investigation, he devised a plan to establish three economic development zones in seven counties. The plan called for nine major development projects. The decision eventually turned the tide, and local residents emerged with greater confidence in their ability to withstand disasters.

Ngari people finally managed to escaped the economic calamity in 1993. However, in February 1994, yet another devastating snowstorm, the most severe in 50 years, hit Ngari. Under Kong's leadership, three relief teams were dispatched to the stricken areas.

Kong's team concentrated on Gegyai and Gerze counties, where they directed the struggle against the storm. Kong established the principle of rescuing people first, livestock second and then restoring production. On February 27, Kong and his team members arrived in Qucang Township, Yarab District, Gerze County. He visited local residents both day and night.

Five days later, Kong had a splitting headache and found it difficult to breathe. Fearing that he would not survive the night, Kong wrote a note to his assistant by the name of Liang, who was sleeping nearby. The note read in part: "Young Liang, I have no idea why I have such a headache and am unable to fall asleep. In case something unfortunate happens to me, please remember not to inform my mother, my wife and my children. Please write a letter informing them I am safe, and please bury me where I fall."

Thanks to blessings from the Gods, Kong survived and under his leadership the Ngari people overcame the adverse effects of the snow storm in only two months. Not a single person died from cold and huger.

Last Days

Kong was a strongly built man, much taller than the average person. Prior to embarking on his first mission to Tibet, Kong requested that a local calligrapher write a scroll which read: "As a man seven chi (equal to 2.33 meters) tall, I am prepared to sacrifice my life in an alien land."

On November 14, 1994, Kong led a delegation into the neighboring Xinjiang Uygur Autonomous Region. Kong never for a minute forgot the farmers and herdsmen in Ngari.

The delegation reached Urumqi, the capital of Xinjiang, on the 19th. Over the next three days, Kong and his colleagues participated in business talks with their Xinjiang counterparts. Thanks to their efforts, a special meeting was held to discuss how Xinjiang could assist Ngari in its economic development effort. A decision was made that beginning in 1995, Xinjiang and other parts of China would supply Ngari with 2 million kg of rice, as well as 3,610 tons of refined cooking oil priced much lower than the true market price. Xinjiang was to also supply 500 tons of liquefied gas.

At 9:30 on the morning of November 29, Kong and his delegation, departed Karamay City on a fact-finding mission to Tacheng. Snow was falling and road conditions were treacherous. However, just prior to reaching Tule County the car was involved in an accident which took the life of Kong. A man loved deeply by the Tibetans had met his untimely demise. Tibetans were deeply saddened by the shocking news. The true fact is that Kong's love for Tibetans has served as an inspiration spurring other people to follow in his footsteps.

Issue: No.4, 1995.

5

A FARMER MILLIONAIRE IN GONGBO GYAMDA

Text by Zhang Bian

Millionaires are numerically many in China's hinterland. In Tibet, however, Goinqog Cering, 42, is perhaps one of a few.

Business-minded

In the 1970s, Gyiba Village cried wolf at the door, with the able-bodied laborers making no more than 30 yuan a month. Whenever there was a natural disaster, the sum would reduce to less than 20 yuan monthly.

At that time, Goinqog Cering lived with his mother-in-law, brother-in-law and sister-in-law. His family belongings included one bronze stove, two sets of beddings and nothing more. Although they could feed themselves, they didn' t have enough butter and meat.

In 1981, when Tibet began to follow the policy which allowed farmers to contract to till land, Goinqog Cering's family was allotted 0.4 hectare of land, one cow and one *piennu* (off-spring of a bull and a female yak) and four horses. Given insufficient input in farming, the per-hectare yield was a mere 750 kg.

Life was not bad for Goinqog Cering, since he had a monthly salary

Goinqog Cering (Right 2) and his truck.

amounting to 300 yuan as a forestry worker.

"One should not be content with one's situation." said Goinqog Cering. "So I quit my job as a forestry worker.

"I loaned some 6,000 yuan from the bank and, with the sum. I purchased a four-ton truck.

"When my old truck moved into the village, many gazed at the giant monster with great curiosity and said I was crazy.

"Today, however, I am rich. "

New Wealth

In 1988, Goinqog Cering sold his old truck and bought a new one at the cost of 30,000 yuan.

In 1989, he sold his truck and bought a Dongfeng truck at the cost of 54,000 yuan.

In 1995, he went to Chengdu where he spent 180,000 yuan for an eight-ton Model 135 Dongfeng truck.

In 11 years, Goinqog Cering made one million yuan, an astronomical figure for most Chinese.

Goinqog Cering has built a two-storey building with large windows. In the spacious sitting-room is a large color TV and a radio cassette recorder. In the warehouse are 2,000 kg of quality rice, wheat flour and highland barley.

Selfless

Goinqog Cering was the first in his village to strike a rich. But he was very much concerned with the poor life of his fellow villagers.

For 11 years running, he always gives ride to passers-by whenever he drives his truce out of or to his village. As a result, people living along the 300-km highway from Lhasa to Conggo Township get to know Goinqog Cering, who never forgets to give food grain to the poor.

When some in his villagers operate small shops for a living, many said to Goinqog Cering, "You have so much money in the bank. You are in a position to run a bigger store," many said to Goinqog Cering.

"You're right," said Goinqog Cering. "I am financially in a position to do so. I can transport everything from Lhasa to sell here. However, if I do so, how can these people get rich?"

Recent years saw establishment of more commercial stores in Gyiba and other villages. More people have become rich.

The Conggo Lake is a holy lake of Tibetan Buddhism. In its middle is an islet with a Buddhist monastery which was out of repair. If the monastery could be repaired, it would attract pilgrims and tourists. Goinqog Cering decided to repair it with money he raised.

In May 1995, department concerned approved his plan. The monastery has been repaired and Goinqog Cering himself spent 120,000 yuan for this purpose.

"Our county got rid of poverty by the end of 1995," said Goinqog Cering who is now a member of the People's Political Consultative Conference of his county. "Under the present situation, it is necessary to seek common wealth. Therefore, efforts should be made to develop collective economy."

Family

Goinqog Cering has five children. "To wipe out poverty permanently, we need to develop education," he said.

"I planned to let my sons to take over my transport business."

"Now, I hope all my children will be able to receive university education."

Issue: No.5, 1996.

6

INTERNATIONAL POSTMAN SHUTTLING BETWEEN SNOW MOUNTAINS

Text & Photo by Zhao Jianwei & Cha Chunming

There is an international post station set up at the China-Sikkim border, called Natoi La mountain pass. It is attached to the Yadong County Post Office of Tibet.

The Natoi La Post Station has an elevation of 4,300 meters. It is sealed off by snow for seven months a year. Nonetheless, Yaling has never suspended his work during the period.

Yaling is the 12th-generation post man of the station. He has since 1989 been delivering international letters free from any charge for several PLA posts in the area.

"As soon as the PLA posts were first set up in 1965, my predecessors started to serve soldiers stationed there," said Yaling.

"It takes four days to complete the journey. I ride horse. Sometimes, however, I ride bicycle.

"Parcels and letters are exchanged every Thursday and Sunday, which should be delivered without mishap and on time. My father raises seven horses in support of my work.

"PLA soldiers are stationed here, far away from their home. I should do

Yaling, an international postman, serves the Sino-Sikkim border area.

the work well to serve them.

"Once I received 15 letters. For the sake of my safety, the Yadong County Post Office advised me to wait for a few days.

"However, I set out on horseback. Half way to my destination, which is 18 km away, I fell into a snow hole which was one meter deep. My legs were hurt. I managed to crawl out of the snow hole, and walked, holding the horse tail in hands, to the PLA post.

"When PLA soldiers there saw I am covered by ice and blood, they were moved to tears.

"For me, it is Ok. It is my work, though I do it free."

Issue: No.1, 1998.

7

DRIVING MY HELICOPTER HOME

— A Visit to Deputy Chief of Staff Leganbo

Text by Zhou Aiming

Kept asking myself whether I would succeed if I interviewed Lobsang Gungbo Leganbo, Deputy Chief of Staff of a PLA air force unit. I had met him at a party a few days earlier, but failed to draw him out as he seemed a rather reticent person.

But when the interview began, he told a most fascinating story. The following is a faithful record.

Joining the PLA Air Force

I was born in 1955 in Nawo Village, Jinlang Township, Heishui County, in Aba Tibetan-Qiang Autonomous Prefecture of Sichuan Province. There were five people in the family, including my grandpa, parents, elder sister and me. In terms of income, we were a middle-class family.

In the early 1970s, the late Premier Zhou Enlai decided to recruit 100 aircraft pilots from ethnic groups to help solve transportation problems plaguing ethnic areas. Fifty were to be of Tibetan, Qiang, Tu, Hui and Mongolian nationalities, with the remainder to be drawn from the Uygur, Khazark and some other ethnic groups.

In 1973, when I was in middle school third grade, the school authorities arranged for 36 students to go for a physical examination. We were told that those who passed would be recruited as aircraft pilots in service of the locality.

Joining the PLA air force, however, involved strict physical requirements. Everyone had to weigh at least 50 kg. My height of 1.6 meters was acceptable, but my weight of 49 kg was just below the standard.

As I met all the other physical requirements, the local authorities decided to move me to study in the county middle school some 60 km from my home. I stayed there for three months. During this time, I received special care in study and diet. The chef dispatched to do cooking for me prepared everything I liked, with each meal including three dishes and one soup. In the end, my weight soared to 58 kg.

Our county had a population of 100, 000. O'mo Zenam (now a regiment commander-level pilot) and I were the only ones to be recruited. An editor with the *PLA Air Force Daily* wrote a TV play depicting our experience, including how we were recruited.

School Study

We were rushed, by train, to Hami in Xinjiang from Chengdu in Sichuan, and it took us three days and three nights. The weather was foul. Strong winds whipped pebbles into the air to lash our faces. Xinjiang in Tibetan means desert. In our eyes, here was a truly dry land. I kept asking myself whether I could survive in such a place.

We were divided into two brigades, with one brigade composed of trainees from Xinjiang living down stairs and those of Tibetan origin staying upstairs.

The school offered nutritious food of different tastes. In the beginning, however, I disliked crabs and prawns. In my hometown, we even shunned eggs, fish and chicken. During festivals at home, we slaughtered sheep. But they were not cooked on that day, as we Tibetans tend to think that these sheep are not thoroughly dead until the following day. In time, however, I grew to love the food as it was not only nutritious but also very tasty.

Leganbo.

We underwent classroom studies for 18 months. This was closely followed by flight lessons. The school organized translators for us. As I was from Sichuan, my Chinese was comparatively much better than other Tibetans students. This proved a boon in study.

Solo Flight

Finally, on July 16, 1975, it was my turn to fly solo. Previously, I had always had a tutor at my side when flying, but I had longed to be alone. When the chance came, my heart beat violently.

It was a fine day. My plane brought up the rear. Suddenly, one of the planes ahead failed to make a good turn. This forced us to improvise before eventually making a sharp turn.

Upon landing, the school authorities spoke highly of our prompt reaction. Our solo flight turned out to be a success.

After this, the trainees were divided into three groups. One group graduated to fly transport aircraft, the second to fly the interceptors, while my group was to fly helicopters. We were sent to Zuxian County (present-day Zuzhou City) in June 1976 for another year of advanced lessons. On graduation in June 1977, I was assigned to be a pilot of the PLA Chengdu Military Area.

Meritorious Deeds

Over the years, I have flown four kinds of planes for a total of 3,000-plus hours. They included the Black Eagle and Mig-17. I love to be a pilot. It is the CPC and the Chinese Government who raised me form being the son of a farmer in a mountainous area to a PLA pilot.

After 1983, I was on several emergency missions, including recovering a space satellite, flood control, rescuing injured people, earthquake relief work in Yunnan, assistance to frontier work in Tibet and aerial survey.

In June 1986, I was ordered to ship power station equipment and medicine weighing several hundred tons to Medog, a remote part of Tibet.

In 1988, when the forest on the China-Nepal border caught fire, I carried a party of forest fire experts and leaders of Tibet Autonomous Region for a survey. That is a high place, with an elevation of 5,000 meters. Our successful mission led to prompt efforts to put out the forest fire.

In 1994, I worked closely with a state ministry surveying northern Tibet. For more than two months, I flew in an area notorious for its high elevation, scarcity of oxygen and fierce weather.

The past few years saw sharp increase in the number of foreigners in Tibet. There were cases when some German and British visitors were caught in a difficult weather conditions and I was sent to rescue them.

For all that I have done, I was repeatedly granted awards, including three third-class awards and one second-class award.

Homebound Flight

During the Flower Festival on August 15, 1995, a flat terrace was built for the arrival of Leganbo's helicopter. For centuries, people had seen eagles flying in the sky. They never expected to see a metallic eagle up there, and so had gathered around the terrace from early morning. To their disappointment, however, bad weather forced him to cancel the mission.

On September 16, however, Leganbo got another chance. It was a fine day, and he flew over the highway flanked by villages, bringing the helicopter down low so that all the villagers could see him.

Against the backdrop of spotless blue sky, Leganbo's helicopter hovered over his village. Down there, the villagers chanted prayers. Originally, the villagers refused to believe Leganbo could fly. Now they could see it in reality. As the helicopter landed and the local hero climbed out, the villages also came to admire this unique event in local history.

Leganbo flew back home again the following June, when he was sent to survey the forest fire situation in a border area. His helicopter circled the village several times.

From then on, whenever there were helicopters flying in the sky, the villagers thought Leganbo had come back. They would bring out highland barley wine and white *khada* scarves, shouting loudly: "Leganbo, please come and have a taste!"

Sometimes, Leganbo dropped bottled mineral water and biscuits to the villagers as gifts. The villagers cherished then so dearly, however, that they were left as the Buddhist shrine for worship.

"They came from the Heaven, where Buddha lives," one villagers said.

Contribution to Hometown

My fellow villagers had been carrying water on their backs for generations before a drinking water project was undertaken.

It took them about two hours to make a round trip. I brought the matter up with the PLA leaders in our regiment. It was finally decided that pipes would be erected to channel water from the source some 3 km away.

I am also planning to set up a buffalo farm. Yaks are not suitable for farming in my hometown, at an elevation of 2,900 meters. Buffalos, however, will be a valuable help for my fellow villagers.

Happy family life

In January1955, Leganbo was born. The following August, Luo Yingchu was born. Both families were wild with happiness. Even before the two babies were born, their grandmothers had decided that they would marry when they grew up.

The two children went to the same school, studying in the same class. Their relationship was known to all, so that they were often the subject of jokes. Upon graduation, she went to teach in a local school, and they saw each other at weekends.

Luo was good at singing and dancing. She worked with might and main, and finally was promoted to be secretary of the Heishui County committee of the Communist Youth League. Later, she worked as the director of the County Archives.

Leganbo went back home to marry in 1980. The whole village celebrated their wedding for three days and three nights.

After the marriage, she moved from Heishui County to Chengdu, where she worked as director of the

Presidential Office of the Sichuan Provincial Political and Legal Institute.

The couple have two sons. The eldest, Lexiang, is 15, and the younger, Luo Wei, is 10. The family leads a happy life.

Issue: No.2, 1998.

8

MY FRIENDS IN DONGGAR TOWNSHIP

Text by Liao Dongfan

EDITOR'S NOTE: On the eve of celebrating the 40th anniversary of the Democratic Reform in 1959 in Tibet, the author cannot help miss friends he made during his 24 years of contact with the region.

Beginning in the mid-1960s, I shuttled between villages in Donggar Township, Doilungdeqen County, in the western suburbs of Lhasa. I remained there for four years, and have since maintained close correspondence with some of them.

Namgyai: Fate of Three Generations

I came to know Namgyai in the winter of 1965, during a four-year period when I was engaged in cultural undertakings in Tibet. As I could speak Tibetan after a fashion, and knew the traditional art form of the region, I was sent to train a performing team organized by local farmers, led by Namgyai.

The Democratic Reform abolishing feudal serfdom had fired the enthusiasm of farmers for both production and cultural entertainment. Performing teams mushroomed in the area, and the Donggar Farmers' Performing Team was just one of them.

The author (Left 2) with Namgyai and his family.

During the day, we worked in the fields together. In the evening, we gathered in the township primary school for rehearsal. All of the team members were good at singing and dancing, and cherished a strong interest in appearing on stage.

The team performed items created by farmers themselves. They told of new things and new situations they were experiencing. In two months, we created a good repertoire, which was performed on the eve of the 1965 New Year's Day in the Doilungdeqen County government office compound. Our performance turned out to be a great success, drawing roars of laughter and hearty applause.

Working day and night with the performing team made it possible to make friends with team members, Namgyai had a family of four: wife, four-year-old daughter and mother-in-law. Years later, he had a second daughter.

I often visited Namgyai at his home. Believe it or not, he lived in a house without any windows. During cooking, the house was filled with suffocating smoke. At this point of time, he would invite me out of the house for a breath of fresh air. I advised him to move, but he told me he got the house during the Democratic Reform, and thought it much better than his previous life in the open air.

At my request, he described his life:

"My father was a herder in Ranbanam Mountain Gully. Driven by poverty, he refused to pay taxes. The local authorities tied him to a horse's tail and exiled him to Donggar, where he was welcomed with 100 lashes.

"At that time, I was aged 10. When I begged my way to Donggar, Father had already been beaten black and blue. I stayed with him in the jail. According to local law, inmates were not to be given any food, and had to beg for it themselves.

"Naturally, I was the source of food supply.

"I spent years in the jail, and my hair was filled with fleas. I was itching all over, but refrained from killing them as Buddhism bans killing any creature. If I killed the fleas, Father would have been responsible. I endured such hardships, and became a flea man in the end, whom others shunned.

"I became a slave for the Donggar magistrate at 14. In 1956, Father was released, but died soon afterwards. I was then transferred to be the slave of another county magistrate. In 1958, my master was transferred to work in Lhakang in Lhoka. In 1959, the armed rebellion broke out in Tibet. My master fled to Bhutan after the rebellion was put down. I didn't go, and joined the PLA and followed the troops back to Donggar.

"I was active during the Democratic Reform. My fate changed. I won personal freedom and was given land, cows, sheep and house. Before long, I married an ex-serf named Enzhub and had our first daughter Zhasang.

"I try my best to be a good husband, a good father and a good performing team leader."

In the 1980s, Namgyai became the Head of Donggar Township and Secretary of the CPC Township Committee. Leaving that smoky dwelling, he built a new house north of the meeting place of the Qinghai-Tibet and Lhasa-Zetang Highways.

I saw much of Namgyai when I was on an errand in Tibet in July 1997. In his home, with 300 square meters of floor space, there are household electrical appliances, electric lamps and telephones. He has also built two houses leased to people from outside Donggar. Namgyai and his wife till 0.5 hectare of farmland harvesting some 3,000-kg of grain a year. As he was a local government official, he enjoys a monthly pension.

Namgyai's retirement is filled with luster. He does farm labor, enjoys warm sunlight through the glass windows of his home, breathes fresh air in the courtyard, listens to radio programs and watches TV while sipping buttered tea. Sometimes, he goes out to chat with old villagers.

Zhasang, the eldest daughter, is good at both Chinese and Tibetan. She is now the Secretary of the CPC Donggar Committee, exercising leadership over some 1,000 households.

Benba, the younger daughter, graduated from middle school in 1984, and later studied in the Tibet Institute for Nationalities for two years.

"Donggar people enjoy an average income of 1,500 yuan a year. But, some villages in the remote mountainous area in the county, however, are still in poverty. I will do my best to help lift them out of the water," said Zhasang.

Puncog Cering: What to Do After Becoming Rich

When Namgyai was the performing team leader, Puncog Cering was the manager. He is about the same age with Namgyai, and is married to a sister of Namgyai's wife.

When the Donggar Farmers' performing Team was founded, members had to prepare everything needed for a performance. This situation lasted until Puncog Cering became its manager. He organized the team members to reclaim wasteland and the grain thus harvested was mostly sold to the State for cash that was used to buy things indispensable for the team.

Later, Puncog Cering was elected leader of his production team, chief of the local tractor station and principal of the Donggar Primary School.

During his eight years as production team leader, local grain production doubled. When he was the tractor station chief, the station had surplus money to give bonuses to its members, and Puncog Cering used his share to buy a black-and-white TV.

During the reform and opening, which started in the late 1970s throughout China, Puncog Cering reacted positively. He organized some 20 farmers to form an Agriculture-Industry-Commerce Production Group, which operated independently from the production team. It owned tractors, threshers and other farming tools, and opened stores, restaurants and processing workshops.

One year later, the team made a profit of 80,000 yuan. For the first time in their history, team members possessed 10,000 yuan, a sum coveted by most of the Chinese then. Puncog Cering was elected model worker at the Lhasa, Tibetan and even national levels. He was sent to visit Beijing and other parts of China.

Upon his return home, he bought a mini-bus for a passenger transport business. He also organized green-house production of vegetables and joined hands with Xindu County in Sichuan Province in running a hardware store and a *khada* scarf factory.

In 1994, when I was in Lhasa attending the ceremony marking the completion of repairs to the Potala Palace, I visited both Namgyai and Puncog Cering. We were happy to see each other. Puncog Cering had built a spacious house furnished with a color TV set and Tibetan furniture.

"I make now 30,000 to 50,000yuan," he said. "What should I do with this money? I will send my children to study in universities. If it is possible, I will send them to study abroad!"

Now, Puncog Cering has attained his goal. His eldest daughter has graduated from the Tibet Institute for Nationalities and is an official with Doilungdeqen County. His second daughter has finished her graduate study in the Sichuan Huaxi Medical University, and is working for the Health Commission of the Tibet Autonomous Region's government. His first son has finished his study in the Computer Department of Chongqing University, and is an assistant professor with the Tibet Farming and Livestock Breeding Institute, while the second son is studying in the Southwest Minzu University in Chengdu. His stepdaughter has graduated from the Tibet Agriculture and Livestock Breeding College and is now a technician with the Lhasa Chicken Farm.

Issue: No.2, 1999.

9
LAND WHICH I WILL NEVER FORGET

Text by Wang Lu

The writer is not Tibetan, but she is obsessed with the blue sky, snowy mountains, rivers and grasslands in that part of the world. What's more, she misses those who cared for her there, and all those whom she takes as brothers and sisters.

I went to Tibet after having finished university study in 1960. During that period, I came to know many Tibetans, including my house landlady and an old man who showed me loving care. I lost my parents when young, and it was these people who brought me family warmth again. I have always regarded them as my kind parents in mind.

My Tibetan Mom

I began working as an editor for the *Tibet Daily* in 1960. In 1962, I got an assignment to cover a rural story. It was my first trip to a village.

I arranged to live with an old Tibetan lady. She was very glad to see a young woman, and treated me with great warmth and tea and wine.

When told I had a newborn daughter, hot tears rolled down her wrinkled

Wang Lu, the author with her Tibetan mother.

cheeks.

This was a tattered house, and the family comprised many children huddled in a few rooms. Seeing I was timid woman, the old lady kept waiting for my return home no matter how late it was. Every evening, when I came close to the house, I shouted: "Aunt!" The house dog echoed my call by barking. And the old lady came out to greet me, keeping calling: "Don't worry! Don't fear!"

Entering the house, she often took out a wheat cake from her bosom and inserted it into my cold hands.

Once I fell ill, she pleaded with me to get some exposure from sunlight atop the house. It is the Tibetans' belief that sunlight has a curative effect on all illness.

When I had to leave for *Tibet Daily*, the old lady impressed me with a sense of loss. As my car moved away into the far distance, she was still standing stop a high terrace, still waving. Though I could not see her clearly, I was sure that she had tears on her cheeks!

My Tibetan Parents

I am not Tibetan, but I have many Tibetan moms and dads. Frankly speaking, they were my house landlords whom I came to know when I was put up with them during my field work.

They treated me as their dear daughter, and missed me when I returned to my work unit. Once, when I was covering a meeting of Lhoka prefectural government leaders, one worker came during an interval, and told me: "Your mother has come."

Wow! How could this woman of Han nationality, whose parents died many, many years ago, have a mother? Many wondered, and were even astonished to hear this.

When this "mother" came in, they found it was an old Tibetan woman carrying some Tibetan food in both hands. She was my landlady in Qoingyai.

As a matter of fact, I have many Tibetan mothers and Tibetan fathers. Very often, they visited me in Lhasa, where I worked for the *Tibet Daily*.

During a Tibetan New Year, one of my Tibetan fathers drove a horse and visited me at my house. He brought me butter, *zanba* (roasted highland barley flour, which is the staple food of the Tibetans) and beef. I was happy to experience this paternal warmth, and prepared gifts for him and his wife in the capacity of a Tibetan daughter......

My Tibetan Sisters

Wherever I went, I always had many girls following me. We chatted and laughed endlessly, and they treated me as their real sister.

On a cold fall day of 1962, the Tibetans had just completed harvesting and I was on my way to a local government office. It was cold, and I felt chilly on horseback. In the small house that evening, I was awakened by a sharp pain in the stomach. I didn't have any medicine and suffered also from vomiting and a diarrhea.

When Nyima, with the local government office, was told of the news, she rushed to my house and cleaned for me. After this, she brought me a hot cup of water and inserted a cushion behind my back, I felt really good after this.

When I was sent to work in Shigatse, I had problem satisfying my stomach because I was conceiving then. Seeing this, a Tibetan woman sent me a bag of milk dregs which were my favorite.

My Tibetan Brothers

For a woman, it its really somewhat romantic riding a horse and running in the wilderness while singing and laughing. I loved to do this, too.

Once, I went on horseback to do field work in a rural area. I came across a Tibetan house. The animal stopped suddenly and, no matter what I tried to do, he refused to move even an inch.

At this point, a dog jumped out of the house and ran away, and the horse moved again. I realized that the horse feared the dog. Once in a deep mountain, I had the same experience, and the dog kept barking, and tried to bite us. It was really scaring. At this time, there were Tibetan young men on the slope who shouted at me: "Don't worry!" This was closely followed with stones flying at the dog. Seeing the dog running away with its tail between its legs, I kicked the horse belly and we ran away without even thanking these Tibetans, to my regret today.

Issue: No.4, 1999.

10

MOVING OUT OF AN ARISTOCRAT FAMILY

— The Story of Tangmei Gungjor Baimo

Text by Lhamoco

EDITOR'S NOTE: Tangmei Gungjor Baimo, the former Vice-Chairwoman of the Tibet Committee of the Chinese People's Political Consultative Conference, is a celebrity in Tibet. In the early days after the peaceful liberation of Tibet in 1951, she moved out of an aristocrat family in order to work in the public interest.

On an autumn afternoon last year, as the drizzling rain created numerous ripples on the surface of the Lhasa River in Lhasa, we visited a house close by.

Offspring of The 7th Dalai Lama

We paid a visit to Tangmei Gungjor Baimo, who was born in 1920 into an aristocrat family in Litang, Sichuan Province. The 7th Dalai Lama was a member of her clan, known as Sangzhub Phodrang. When the Sangzhub Phodrang moved to Lhasa, the clan became very influential in the city largely because of the influence of the 7th Dalai Lama.

The author with Tangmei Gungjor Baimo at her home.

Tangmei Gungjor Baimo when young.

"I started to learn to read and write when I was six," said Tangmei Gungjor Baimo. "I was sent to a private school for further study at 11, although in those days most aristocrats were reluctant to let their daughters learn more." "Married at 17. My husband also came from an aristocrat family. We had two daughters and one son. Unfortunately, our son died young. My husband also later died. I remarried, and my husband, Tangmei Toindui Cering, had two sons. The six of us formed a new family."

Teaching Tibetan

In 1951, Tibet won peaceful liberation and the 18th Corps of the Chinese People's Liberation Army (PLA) entered Lhasa. The 18th Corps organized a "cadres' school," and needed people to teach Tibetan.

"I was invited to serve as a Tibetan teacher," said Tangmei Gungjor Baimo. "I hesitated because my husband was an official with the Gaxag, the local government of Tibet, but in the end I went. The officers and men of the

18th Corps lived in tents, and students of the cadres'school studied in the open and also in tents when it rained. They ate black beans and qingke barley. In spite of the difficulties they faced, they studied very hard."

Tangmei Gungjor Baimo's move aroused objections in Lhasa. In 1957, when a reactionary armed organization was formed, they cursed her in the street, and even threw stones at her. However, she persisted with her teaching.

Joining the Women's Association

In 1953, when the Patriotic Women's Association was formed in Lhasa, Tangmei Gungjor Baimo joined and first served as the association's secretary, working hard to free women from the yoke of feudalism.

The association organized parties and anti-illiteracy classes. Association members also gave information on everyday hygiene to Tibetan women.

Received by Chairman Mao

Tibet organized its first group of women to visit Beijing in 1956. Tangmei Gungjor Baimo was one of the 47 members of the group, which visited Beijing, Tianjin, Shanghai, and Wuhan.

In Beijing, Chairman Mao met the group, and had a picture taken with them. Tangmei Gungjor Baimo was excited by these events.

Elected Vice-Chair-Woman

In June 1960, when the Tibet Women's Association was formed, Tangmei Gungjor Baimo served as its Vice-Chairwoman.

In August 1982, she was elected Vice-Chairwoman of the CPPCC Tibet Committee and continued to work hard for the development of Tibet. She retired from the post in 1998.

Now in her 80s, this famous woman enjoys the twilight of her life with her children and grandchildren, and the respect of the public.

Issue: No.2, 2000.

11

LIFELONG STORY OF THE LIVING BUDDHA CHAZHUB NGAWANG LOBSANG

Text by Wen Shi

The Living Buddha Chazhub Ngawang Lobsang was born in 1880 (the Tibetan Year of Iron Dragon) in the noble family of Deleg Raodainba in Shigatse. He died in 1957 as the deputy editor-in-chief of *Tibet Daily* in 1957.

Chazhub Ngawang Lobsang was tonsured to the Sera Monastery in 1885, at the age of five. Before long, he was determined as the reincarnated soul boy of the Living Buddha Gandain Chiba Lobsang Geleg. The enthronement ceremony was held in 1886 in the monastery for him to become the Living

Chazhub Ngawang Lobsang.

Buddha Chazhub Ngawang Lobsang.

The Living Buddha Chazhub Ngawang Lobsang was very intelligent and studied very hard. He won the highest Buddhist academic degree of Lharanba Geshi when he was 21 years old. After this, he travelled around in Tibet, seeking further study of history, literature, poems, Tibetan medicine and astronomy. He was well versed in literature, poems and Tibetan grammar.

The Living Buddha Chazhub Ngawang Lobsang once accompanied the 13th Dalai Lama to visit Beijing, where they were received by Qing Dynasty (1644–1911) Emperor Guangxu. Upon return to Tibet, the 13th Dalai Lama sent him to Japan. Later he served as the sutra teacher for the 14th Dalai Lama, and joined hands with Geshi Xerab Gyamco to collate *Tripitaka*.

At the end of 1951, when the PLA troops were stationed in Lhasa, the Living Buddha Chazhub Ngawang Lobsang, excited at the change, assisted the PLA in social work. At the beginning, the 71-year-old Living Buddha sewed as the vice-president of the Party School for Cadres of the PLA Tibet Military Area. He compiled teaching materials and taught in person.

In 1952, when the Compilation and Examination Committee of the PLA Tibet Military Area was founded, the Living Buddha Chazhub Ngawang Lobsang, then 72 years old, served as an executive committee member. He worked for the publication of the *Tibetan News Release*.

At that time, a small number of people on the upper echelon of the ruling class in Tibet were working hand in glove with pro-imperialists to undermine the implementation of the *Agreement Between the Central Government and the Local Government of Tibet for Methods on the Peaceful Liberation of Tibet*, known as the 17-Article Agreement. The Living Buddha Chazhub Ngawang Lobsang stood firmly by the Central Government, working hard to defend the unification of the motherland. Joining hands with some other major scholars in Tibet, he translated many materials from Chinese to Tibet, and vice versa. As not many books on Tibetan terminology and Tibetan grammar were available at that time, the Living Buddha Chazhub Ngawang Lobsang worked out a book titled *Tibetan Grammar by Chazhub*.

During that period of time, the Living Buddha Chazhub Ngawang

Lobsang served also as a member of the Tibet Patriotic Youths Federation, Board Chairman and Vice-President of the Lhasa Serxing Primary School, and Tibetan language lecturer with the Party School for Cadres of the PLA Tibet Military Area. In 1956, the year before his death, he took up the post as a Tibetan language teacher for the Journalism Training Program of the *Tibet Daily*. He worked very hard. When advised to take it easy, he said: "Yes I am old now. Now, with the presence of the CPC and the Central Government led by Chairman Mao Zedong, I don't feel too tired. I think I am young."

The Living Buddha Chazhub Ngawang Lobsang said at the first anniversary of the founding of the *Tibet Daily*. "Chairman Mao and the CPC are great. Had it not been for them, Tibet would not be peacefully liberated, and the Tibetan people would not be able to get rid of the yoke of imperialism and enjoy equality in the big Chinese family."

In the seven years of his working for the *Tibetan News Release* (predecessor of the *Tibet Daily*), the paper suffered from strong objection from some lamas with the three major monasteries in Lhasa (referring to the Zhaibung, Sera and Gandain Monasteries). Out of his lore for Tibet and for the motherland at large, the Living Buddha Chazhub Ngawang Lobsang persisted in delivering the paper to the three monasteries and explained in great detail the policies of the CPC and the Central Government to lamas there. When he became the deputy editor-in-chief of the *Tibet Daily* he did this until his death.

In 1954, the Qinghai-Tibet and the Sichuan-Tibet Highways were open to traffic. Elated as he was, the Living Buddha Chazhub Ngawang Lobsang wrote a poem titled *Jade Belts and Golden Bridge*, which was loved by the Tibetans. The poem read in part:

"High mountains piercing into the sky like heavenly pillars,
Gallop thousands of miles like surging waves of the ocean;
Deep ravines and rapids cut off Tibet's connection
with neighboring provinces of Qinghai and Xikang,
With upturned cliffs which are sharp and steep.

To cross these ravines and piercing peaks,
Even holy eagles have worries.
To build a road which links Tibet with the outside world,
Heroic builders brave fierce wind and high rains,
Drink lukewarm water and eat half done food."

On September 30, 1957, it drizzled in Lhasa. Editors with the *Tibet Daily* had begun working in the morning, but they could not find their deputy editor-in-chief. Where was the Living Buddha Chazhub Ngawang Lobsang?

At the time when the paper leaders were making arrangement for young staff to find the old man, they received a report that the Living Buddha Chazhub Ngawang Lobsang was attacked by a mad lama. They rushed to the spot and sent the old man to the Lhasa People's Hospital.

The Living Buddha Chazhub Ngawang Lobsang didn't recover, and demised at 1: 59 pm on December 1.

Just a few days before his death, the Living Buddha Chazhub Ngawang Lobsang told visiting leaders with the Tibet Work Committee of the Central Government: "My lifelong experience told me that only by following the leadership of the CPC and Chairman Mao, only upholding unity, patriotism and progress, and only opposing separatism, can Tibet have a bright future."

Issue: No.1, 2000.

12

"SERVING MY HOMETOWN WITH KNOWLEDGE I HAVE LEARNED"

— An Interview With Tibet's First Weather PhD Xudo

Text by Wang Yuanhong

Dr. Xudo

Xudo, a Tibetan, was born in November 1969.

In July 1985, he went to study atmospheric monitoring in the Nanjing Weather College.

In July 1990, he was given a job in the Weather Broadcasting Bureau of Tibet Autonomous Region.

In August 1995, he was transferred to do scientific research in the Tibet Plateau Atmospheric Environment Science Research Institute.

In September 1998, he went to study for an MA and later for a PhD in the Geo-Science and Resources Research Institute of the Chinese Academy of Sciences.

In 2003, he returned to the Tibet bureau as Tibet's first PhD in the weather field.

Xudo had an opportunity to work in Beijing, a city with better living and working conditions, but he chose to return home.

"I will serve my hometown with the knowledge I have learned," he said without hesitation.

In 1985, Xudo received a letter from the Nanjing Weather College, informing him he had been accepted to study in the college. He was only 16.

He was happy and so were his parents. However, where could he get money to cover his study in Nanjing? His parents sold a draught cow, and he left home with 200 Yuan in his pocket.

With this sum, and with allowances given by the college and subsidies from his uncle who taught in Tibet, he eked out a living and grew into a Tibetan scholar who was good enough to write papers in Chinese after five years. He is also good at English.

Xudo won his BA in July 1990 and was given a job at the Weather Station of Tibet Autonomous Region in September, engaging in the reception and analysis of NOAA satellite pictures of clouds.

He worked very hard and performed excellently; he also succeeded in monitoring forest fires and mountainous snowstorms.

At the end of 1991, Xudo was charged with the task of monitoring the environment in the three-rivers area. From 1991 to 1995, he coordinated with specialists with the Remote Sensing Institute of the Chinese Academy of Sciences to conduct four field studies in 18 counties (cities) covering some 60,000 square km.

In 1995, Xudo was transferred to the Tibet Plateau Atmospheric Environment Science Research Institute. There, he plunged into the study of ways and means of monitoring snowstorms in Tibet, a project sponsored by the Tibet Weather Broadcast Station, and was put in charge of studying materials related to snowstorm in accordance with the NOAA satellite cloud pictures. In order to gain real knowledge, he went to Damxung to survey the snow that had accumulated over the years. His research won a third class award for scientific progress in the region.

Dr. Xudo and his collegues.

In 1996, the Tibet Commission of Science and Technology decided to undertake study of the ozone layer and ultra-violet ray radiation in the Tibetan plateau in accordance with the suggestion made by Xudo. He and a Norwegian expert installed a multi-wave ozone and ultra-violet ray radiation meter on the top of the Tibet Weather Bureau, and he himself took in charge of the receiving and analyzing the data.

In four years, he used materials generated by the meter and materials supplied by the Lhasa Weather Broadcast Station to complete his analysis whilc studying for an MA in the Chinese Academy of Sciences. He finished his 100,000-word thesis with great success. The project he undertook passed the examination of the Tibet Commission of Science and Technology.

Xudo should be counted as a young scientist enjoying success, but he still felt he fell short of society's needs. This drove him to further study in 1998. He passed all the examinations for PhD study in the Beijing Graduate School of the Chinese Science and Technology University.

His English study encountered many hurdles in the first year, but he hit the books with might and main and even employed a tutor. Eventually, he caught up with others in English study.

During his study in Beijing, Xudo continued his own research. Form April to June 2001, he visited the Tromso Research Institute of the Norwegian Weather Bureau for two months, conducting academic exchanges. He delivered a report entitled *Tibet Plateau and Weather in Tibet*. His introduction of the traditional Tibetan culture, the Tibet Weather Bureau and the climatic features in the Tibet Plateau aroused great interest among his Norwegian colleagues.

Xudo has published more than 10 treatises in *Atmospheric Science* and some other academic journals. In 1998, he was cited as a national model for others to emulate.

Issue: No.3, 2003.

13
DORGAR PUNCOG RAOGYI AS I KNOW HIM

Text by Wang Furong

During the time of the Tubo Kingdom in the 7th century, the ancestors of Dorgar Puncog Raogyi assisted Tibetan King Songtsen Gambo in governing.

In 728 Cering Wanggyi, forefather of Dorgar Puncog Raogyi tracing back nine generations, was appointed a Galoon official, the first time the Dorgar family had held such a post in the Gaxag government of Tibet. Cering Wanggyi was both a politician and an excellent Tibetan scholar, who finished the *Biography of Pholhanas*, *Biography of Galoon Officials* and the Tibetan famous literary work *Xunnu Darmai*, which are still popular today.

Over the succeeding two centuries, there were five persons of the Dorgar family who had became Galoon officials in the Gaxag government, and Puncog Raogyi became the sixth. Among the known noble families, the Dorgar family provided the largest number of Galoon officials.

In 1903, Dorgar Puncog Raogyi was born, being sent to a noble school for his education at the age of six.

In 1922 the 19-year-old Dorgar became an official of the local government of Tibet, and later he was the first chief Tibetan police officer of Lhasa Police Station, secretary of the Gaxag government, magistrate of Cona County of Lhoka, and a regimental commander of the Tibetan army prior to the

The Tibetan delegation sent to attend the National Day celebration in Beijing reached the capital city by train and air in two groups on September 28, 1953. Picture shows the 54-member Tibetan delegation headed by Dorgar Puncog Raogyi (with a bouquet in hand in the front row) walking out of the Beijing Railway Station. The first left was Lin Boqu, Secretary-General of the Central People's Government, and Li Weihan, Minister in Charge of the Ethnic Minority Affairs Committee of the Central People's Government.

peaceful liberation of Tibet.

In 1950, before the People's Liberation Army (PLA) entered Tibet, the Gaxag government had established a command office for tackling any emergency. The four Galoon officials were reassigned in regard to their responsibilities, with Dorgar Puncog Raogyi being put in charge of the Tibetan army as a regimental commander and the head of Northern Tibet.

Becoming PLA Regimental Commander

On July, 14, 1951 the Central People's Government representative Zhang Jingwu came to the border city of Yadong via India. The next day, three

Galoon officials including Dorgar Puncog Raogyi visited him at Renqengang in Yadong. Mr. Zhang presented to them the policies of the Central People's Government regarding the peaceful liberation of Tibet and the significance of uniting the Han and Tibetan nationalities, jointly constructing Tibet and guarding the frontier of motherland.

Through the patient, thoughtful explanations of Zhang Jingwu and his followers, in addition to the stronger force of the officials of Tibetan Government who supported the 17-Article Agreement, the 14th Dalai Lama finally decided to return to Lhasa after having briefly fled to India. The plot of the imperialists encouraging the Dalai Lama to escape abroad had failed.

In early 1952, the central government decided to set up the PLA Tibet Military Area and to appoint two vice regimental commanders among figures of the Tibetan upper class. Through discussions with the 14th Dalai Lama and the Gaxag government, Ngabo Ngawang Jigme was appointed as the first vice regimental commander and Dorgar Puncog Raogyi the second vice regimental commander in recognition of their significant contribution to the peaceful liberation of Tibet.

However, at this moment, upper class reactionaries led by Sicao Lukangwa and Lobsang Zhaxi, and backed up and instigated by a reactionary organization calling itself the "people's conference", staged a riot. Soikang Wangqen Geleg, a splittist who had just returned Lhasa from India, worked hand in glove with them. In the middle of March 1952, the "people's conference"and Tibetan forces surrounded the house where Zhang Jingwu stayed. Some people like Ngabo, Dorgar and Lhalu did not see eye to eye with those such as Soikang. When Dorgar was told that the Tibetan force involved was the fourth regiment led by his son Soinam Dorbogyi, he flew into a rage and said angrily, "It's totally mischievous! Get them withdrawn quickly!"

Becoming Chairman of Delegation Attending the Ceremony of National Day

In 1953, the Central People's Government decided to arrange the people who followed the 14th Dalai Lama and the 10th Panchen Erdeni to attend the celebration in Beijing to mark the fourth year of the founding of the People's Republic of China.

On October 1, Dorgar and other members of the Tibetan delegation mounted to the platform, watching and inspecting with Great Leader Chairman Mao the troupes of armed forces and processions of the people. Just at this moment, he felt the nation's strength and the people's power.

What he could never forget was the cordial meeting with Chairman Mao and commander-in-chief Zhu De on October 18, when he himself presented the light green, valuable *khada* scarves to them.

Chairman Mao asked them with regard how they were doing after coming to Beijing and whether they had any other requirement. He instructed: "We should unite with various ethnic groups in China. So long as they are Chinese, who are against imperialism and for patriotism and unity, we should unite with them... What the central government can offer to help you it is sure to give you. Helping various ethnic groups in their development and advancement is to the benefit of the whole nation. We are expecting the development and advancement of various ethnic groups."

From the end of the ceremony for National Day to the middle of next June, Dorgar and his companions visited a dozen large cities across China. In late June, Dorgar came to the Central People's Broadcast Station on three consecutive days upon invitation and described over the air waves the cordial talks with Chairman Mao, what he had seen and heard during the grand ceremony for National Day and the visits of various places in China to the Tibetans in Qinghai-Tibet Plateau and each part throughout China as well as the world.

Becoming PCFFOTAR Member

In February 1955, Dorgar Puncog Raogyi took the post of vice regimental commander for the PLA Tibet Military Area. On September 27, Premier Zhou Enlai of the State Council issued a decree to grant Dorgar Puncog Raogyi the military title of PLA lieutenant general. When he received the lofty military title from the hands of Marshal He Long, the eyes of the 52-year-old Tibetan army man brimmed over with warm, excited tears.

In April 1956, the State Council approved the establishment of the Preparatory Committee for the Founding of Tibet Autonomous Region. For this reason, the Central People's Government dispatched a central delegation headed by Marshal Chen Yi, vice premier of the State Council, to Tibet to attend the founding ceremony. The 14th Dalai Lama decided Dorgar Puncog Raogyi as the representative of the local government of Tibet, should accompany Marshal Chen Yi in all his movements throughout Tibet.

Showing His Ability in Diplomatic Affairs

In September 1953, Indian Prime Minister Nehru sent a letter to Premier Zhou Enlai proposing to negotiate on bilateral relations between China and India.

The Central People's Government of China was very concerned with this negotiation and set up a special 11-person "China-India Negotiation Committee" as an instruction unit for the talks. Premier Zhou was the Chairman. Besides related leaders of the Ministry of Foreign Affairs, Yang Gongsu, assistant of foreign affairs and representative of Central People's Government in Tibet, Zhang Guohua and Fan Ming, leaders of Tibet Working Committee participated in the negotiations. The local government of Tibet dispatched Galoon official Dorgar Puncog Raogyi and Garzhang, commander-in-chief of Tibetan forces to participate.

On January 7, 1954, the first plenary conference was held in Beijing. Premier Zhou presided and presented an important speech on the history of exchanges in the China Tibet region between China and India and the stand to be taken by China in the negotiation.

Through negotiations lasting four months, China and India signed agreements covering trade and transportation between China Tibet region and India.

Issue: No.2, 2004.

14

BLIND MUSICIAN AND HIS SONGS

Text by Liao Dongfan

In the first part of the 20th century, Wuxi in Jiangsu Province saw the birth of a blind musician named A Bing.

At about the same time, in far-off Lhasa, there was also a blind musician named Ngajor Namgyi. He initiated a music school for the cultivation of talent and he himself wrote and composed many *Duishie* songs known to all in Tibet. Ngajor Namgyi's songs are still popular but many do not know his name.

Eyes Pecked Away by a Crow

In the spring of 1979, accompanied by Ma Alu a young musician, I went along the Yarlung Zangbo River to study local folk songs and folk traditions. At Lengda Ferry in Gyicha County, we were astonished to find Namgyi, a noted blind musician, who lived in a nearby remote mountainous village. According to local residents, in 1894, Namgyi was born into a poor serf family and his parents had to undertake corvee labor for their lord, leaving their son, Namgyi, inside their locked home. When the boy was two, a large crow suddenly flew down and peeked out his two eyeballs. Namgyi rolled about the earth floor in intense pain. When his parents returned home from work and saw the miserable situation of the child, they felt deep distress. They had to hold him in their arms and could do nothing but cry out and pray to Buddha. Since then sunlight had never appeared in the world of Namgyi. People gave him a name of "Namgyi Gudong", meaning blind Namgyi.

His father played a six-stringed musical instrument very well. The old man decided to teach Namgyi how to play it so that he could have some ability to earn a living. Soon after his death, Namgyi's mother died, too. Since then he has lived alone and played the six-stringed musical instrument and made a living as a performer on the banks of the Yarlung Zangbo River. Namgyi is a very bright person. Although he cannot see the colors of the world, there are various dulcet musical tones flowing in his mind. He can not only play local music but also learned from people crossing the river the music, songs and dances originating from other places in Tibet. No matter what the songs heard from other people, he could play them on his instrument.

Moving to Lhasa

Prof. Xoikang Dagyi of the Music Department of Tibet University once learned music from Namgyi at the age of 13 and gained good knowledge of his life experiences. He said, about 1914 when the 13th Dalai Lama wanted to develop mining in Tibet, the Gaxag government sent a Galoon named Charong Dasang Zhyamdui and the Gaxag government secretary Soikang Toinzhub Dorje (who was Xoikang Dagyi's father) to the region of Gyiacha to inspect the local mining resources. When they passed by the Lengda Ferry, they found this youth, then in his 20s, playing the six-stringed musical instrument very well and decided he was a promising folk artist. They said to this young man: "You are gifted in music. It is a pity that you are in this remote mountainous region. Go to Lhasa...that is the place for you!"

After arriving in Lhasa, Namgyi played his instrument and made a living as a performer in the streets during the day, and at night slept either on the streets or under the roof of monasteries and noble families' homes. At that time, the people in Lhasa loved the music of *Duishie* and *Namma* songs and dances from the Shigatse area and Ngari, *Duishie* featured undulating melodies and robust dance movements, while *Namma* belonged to a kind of ancient palace singing and dancing displaying a beautiful melody and graceful movements.

Namma Gyidu was a folk organization composed of famous musical instrument players of the Tibetan, Hui and Han ethnic groups. The six-stringed instrument, the dulcimer, flute, erheen, jinghu, hitting bell and bunch bell provided the music and by relying solely on these seven kinds of instruments, a small *Duishie* and *Namma* band worthy of its name was organized. Performing at various festivals and on happy occasions became the patent of Namma Gyidu.

Namgyi could only play the music of his hometown as well as a few folk songs of the Gongbo and Kham area, so he could not obtain much recognition from people in Lhasa. He led a lonely and hard life and only had the six-stringed musical instrument left by his father as a companion.

Join Namma Gyidu

During the most difficult time, Soikang Toinzhub Dorje supported him to rent a small house in the Tabaling street area in the eastern part of Lhasa and recommended him to learn *Duishie* and *Namma* music from Namma Gyidu Masters Ngadong Rema (Hui) and Wanggyi.

Namgyi had a kind of outstanding comprehensive ability about music. In addition, as he was blind, he worked harder to learn. Within just a few years, he made great progress. He not only imbibed several compositions of *Duishie* and *Namma*, but also learned how to play the dulcimer, erheen, flute and other instruments. When his hands touched various strings, sweet music flew out like a mountain fountain. It was no wonder that many people exclaimed: "Blind Namgyi has magic in his ten fingers." Thus, Namma Gyidu opened its door to him and accepted him as member of the organization. Namgyi did not feel satisfied with his achievements, however, and learned more music knowledge from Hui artist Ayi Woli and Han master Tan.

Duishie and Namma Craze

When Ngadong Rema and Wanggyi died during the 1930s, Namgyi was elected head of Namma Gyidu. In Lhasa, noble men, merchants, citizens and various artisans went to the Lingka every summer where they sang, danced, and drank to their heart's content. With the coming of winter, noble families had the custom of inviting other families to dinner. So, all year round Namma Gyidu artists were most welcome. Whether at Lingka festivals or at a wassail, they could bring happiness and joy to people.

With Namgyi in charge, Namma Gyidu was able to satisfy the needs of both noble officials and ordinary people. As a result, he became so popular that he was referred to as "Ngajor Namgyi", meaning "Brother Namgyi". Wherever he went, some people would cry "Brother Namgyi" and "Teacher Namgyi" endlessly. A girl named Cering in Lhasa married him and served as his eyes everywhere. Thus, Ngajor Namgyi had more time and energy to engage in musical activities.

In the seventh Tibetan month each year, when the *Shoton* (Sour Milk Drinking) Festival was held in Lhasa, 12 folk Tibetan opera and singing and dancing troupes gathered at the Norbu Lingka, the summer palace of the Dalai Lama, to offer a performance. Every year, Chinpa Tibetan opera troupe would bring some new *Duishie* songs from Ongren and Lharze of the Shigatse region, which were played as interludes during the Tibetan opera to the audiences'delight. Every time Ngajor Namgyi led the musical masters and female singers in Gyidu to the performing site of Chinpa Tibetan opera, the music spread further among the residents of Lhasa. Many of their *Duishie* songs. Such as *Long Ping Mountain*, *North* and *Gamba La Mountain*, were popular all over the holy city and everyone tried to be the first to sing them.

Amateur artists performing at Chengguan District of Lhasa. (1959)

First Musical School in Lhasa

With the promotion of Ngajor Namgyi's fame, more and more people went to his place and learned music and instrument playing from him. He rented two houses in Raose Lane of Barkor Street and established the first musical school in Lhasa.

His students included children of nobility, merchants, ordinary young people and artisans, as well as beggars and vagrants in the streets. Namgyi arranged the sitting position of students in the order of their arrival. The people coming earlier sat in the front and the ones coming later sat behind. Tibet was a society of strict ranking. The lowborn people could not sit together with those of higher birth and had to lower their heads, bend their backs and stick out their tongues to express their humility when meeting those of higher rank. Ngajor Namgyi could act contrary to this because he had some idea about equality.

In the school, anyone who picked up the lessons well could then act as a tutor to others.

Each Saturday, students would report their achievements made during the week to the teacher and the other students. The afternoon of that day was the time for group performance. After having supper, everyone brought his own instrument, went to Barkor Street and offered a performance to Lhasa citizens. Erheen and tiehu hung from their waists, a six-stringed musical instrument hung around their neck, dulcimer was placed on a basket and a beggar was hired to carry this on the back. They played instruments while walking, and would make three circuits of Jokhang Temple to offer some lively performance. Those people who watched their performance would mingle to dance. The residents in the buildings at both sides of the street would open their windows and join in with endless acclamation.

In 1942, Ngajor Namgyi died of illness, only living for 48 years. But the contribution he made to the ethnic music of Tibet and the songs he composed will live forever on Qinghai-Tibet Plateau and become a special favor of all Tibetan people.

Issue: No.3, 2005.

15
THE FIRST FEMALE PROFESSOR OF TIBETAN CULTURE

Text by Yang Enhong

Editor's notes: Dondrup Lhamo, from Sichuan Province, is the first famous female Professor in the early of 20th century in China. She was then called "a cruising eagle over the Qinghai-Tibet Plateau". Prof. Yang Enhong, a scholar of oral epic King Gesar, interviewed her two years ago. Here are excerpts from their talks.

The Earliest Responsibility of a Poor Family

In February 1913 (Tibetan calendar) I was born in a tiny mud hut in a small Town in Sichuan on the Qinghai-Tibet Plateau. My father Deng Kecheng came from Jiang'an of Sichuan and served in the infantry contingent of Zhao Erfeng Corps as a division commander. After moving to Kham, he felt sick of the war but intoxicated with the magnificent landscape, which actually stimulated him to decide to settle down. My mother, Drolma Qinzhu, is an ethnic Tibetan from Batang. Following the orders of my uncle, they tied the knot. When I was born, my father lifted me up in his hands and said proudly: "This is the pearl of my family." Then my mother named me

Professor Dondrup Lhamo is tutoring in a night school.

"Dondrup Lhamo".

In my ninth year, my father passed away due to illness and left my mother to raise me. Life was a struggle as I grew up with my two little siblings. In my childhood, my time was spent working with my mother climbing a mountain for firewood to exchange for food. On hearing of my family's situation, my uncle sent us some Tibetan cash to help my mother. We used the cash to start a small shop in front of our house to help us survive, while my uncle brought us the groceries to sell from his hometown, including walnuts, peaches, dried fruit, butter and so on. I still remember how I helped my mother by slicing butter into small pieces to sell to people from the cities. Actually I always pleased her by doing a good job. The hardships of this life were very hard on my mother. Nevertheless, she never complained and was not discouraged, but rather remained endlessly happy and friendly, typical of ethnic Tibetans. Whenever we had a free moment at night, she liked to share Tibetan folk stories with us or teach us how to sing folk songs and dance of Batang. For us life was hard, but the tiny hut always emitted wonderful music accompanied by our cheers, which I can't forget.

Stepping onto the Road to Seek Knowledge

During that era, Christian missionaries from Britain, the United States and Germany came to Batang and built a Christian community and founded a local school, the Hua Xi School, which I found a ready favorable place to study. It provided accommodation and a medical service. Students were educated from primary to junior middle school. The school was run by a couple from the United States. They spoke very good Tibetan. After being convinced by them of the benefits of sending children to school, my mother sewed a new traditional Tibetan dress for me, washed the canvas bag I had inherited from my father and then sent me to school. That year I was just ten years old but I always remembered my mother's words: person should not be afraid of poverty but should be ashamed of the cowardice of living with no aim in life. The most important issues for a person are firstly food, but the next is knowledge. Although this foreign school had few female students, I guessed that the knowledge we gained would definitely be useful everywhere.

During schooling, my marks in Tibetan and English were always excellent, ranking first in the school (including sports as well). The American couple had a daughter named Rose, the same age as me. She was good at singing and dancing, and fluent in Tibetan. We became very good friends by helping each other. I was born with a good voice. Whenever singing hymns, all foreign teachers and participants in worship were very impressed and always applauded me. I delved into knowledge by taking every opportunity to read as many books and references as possible in my spare time. I dreamed of leaving the mountain area to see the outside world.

In 1935, Hua Xi School had to close for many reasons, and the American couple had to return to their home country. Before leaving they encouraged me to keep on with my studies in the senior high school that was affiliated with the Jin Ling Women's University of Nanjing, if I agreed. Although I was very eager and determined to go to further my knowledge, it was hard to leave my mother and siblings behind when I departed on my journey. What I did not expect was my mother's encouragement that finally motivated me to keep on that journey for knowledge. I made three kowtows in front of my mother, as her child, to pay my respect...and then I followed the trade caravans of Batang to leave for Chongqing. Though I left my mother and my hometown, I did not realize this would be my last chance to see my mother. She passed away before the found of PRC. As transportation and communications were extremely poor during that era, I did not get a chance to see her before she died.

Searching for Knowledge outside the Mountains

In 1930s, there was no road between Sichuan and Tibet. The mountain paths were rough and even very dangerous. I had to follow the trade caravan to trek the massive mountain range. On the way, we crossed over several mountain summits that were 5000 meters above sea level and crossed the Yalong River, Dadu River and others. The merchants were trading while journeying toward Chengdu. Only after three mouths did we reach Chengdu. My husband Li Kai was on the same journey.

In the fall of 1935, having overcome tremendous difficulties, I finally arrived at Nanjing, which was a political, economic and cultural center at that time. With the wife of the American couple's strong recommendation, I was successfully enrolled in Jin Ling High School. The school president was then Wu Yifang. Because I was good at Tibetan, Ms. Huang Yulan, who was also from my hometown, recommended me to be the editor of the monthly journal *Mongolian-Tibetan Journal*. I worked there as a copier and also undertook some proofreading and translation. In my leisure time, I taught Tibetan in the Frontier School.

After the war against Japanese invasion broke out, I followed the transfer of the government offices of the Republic of China by moving to Chongqing. In 1938, I worked as a secretary in Tibetan language and as an oral interpreter in charge of the communication between Chiang Kai-shek and the representative officer of *Gaxag* local government (which had also been moved to Chongqing from Nanjing). Chiang Kai-shek attached great importance to local Tibet. He had proposed to build a road to access Tibet, but the representative of the *Gaxag* local government prevented it. Taking the opportunity while working in Chongqing, I involved myself in learning Tibetan literature from Sherab Gyatso, a well known Qinghai scholar, and Lhodrak Thubten Sangye, the representative of the Tibetan local government. I even worked on translation, collection and study of Tibetan folk songs and stories. *The Takungpao Newspaper* and *Xinmin Evening Newspaper* published all of my achievements under the nom de plume of *Mingzhu*. I also organized the Kham Tibetan Dance Group, consisting of Tibetan students, to deliver performances to the community, which were highly appreciated by various audiences.

I returned to Nanjing after the eight-year war against the Japanese invasion and was formally employed by Zhu Jiahua, the Minister of Education of the Republic of China, as a Tibetan associate professor in the State Political University. I was the first Tibetan associate professor recognized by the public. This was a big event in education circles. A reporter with the surname Zhao conducted an interview with me about this and wrote a paper entitled "Tibetan Eagle-Dondrup Lhamo" in *the Takungpao Newspaper*. Henceforth, I was a quite well known person in Nanjing. In 1946, I participated in a constitutional conference as a prominent person. In 1948, being a woman of Xikang, I undertook the post of representative in the National Congress. During that period, Sherab Gyatso was also in Nanjing as a national congress member. In this period, I worked with government dignitaries, participated in the election campaign for Li Zongren and formed a political relationship with his wife Guo Dejie. I even shared dinner with Shong Meiling and was photographed with her.

In 1949, just before liberation, many key persons of the Republican Government fled to Taiwan, I was asked to go by my friends but I refused and decided to return to my hometown. I believed my roots were there and my future as well.

Being Active in the Exchange between Ethnic Tibetans and Han Chinese

After liberation, I came back to Ya'an, undertaking a government post as the Tibetan secretary for the Cultural and Education Bureau of Xikang Province. I was later invited as Tibetan teacher of Class 13 of the Revolutionary University. In 1951, I was employed as Tibetan teacher for Division 53 of the 18th Army Corps of the People's Liberation Army. I taught officers and soldiers the Tibetan language, while teaching them Tibetan folk songs and introducing them to Tibetan culture. In 1955, I was transferred to the Bureau of Education of Chengdu, Sichuan, where I worked drafting and editing text books in Tibetan language and mathematics. In 1957, Sichuan formed the Ethnic Publishing Press and I was then transferred to that office as editor, while I was also working as a Tibetan language radio broadcaster for the Sichuan People's Broadcasting Station. In 1961, I transferred again to work for the Ethnic Affairs Committee of Sichuan Province.

After the founding of the People's Republic of China, while I was working as a teacher in pursuit of delivering my knowledge to the young generation, I was constantly searching for new knowledge in order to broaden my horizons, including reading a number of ancient Tibetan books. My endless reading and searching enabled me to collect and make comparative studies so that I could provide my students with more knowledge through my teaching. In addition, I took time to translate and edit a number of Tibetan and Chinese books. For instance, I worked together with Tashi Tsering to publish the books entitled *Tibetan Folk Songs* and *Stories of Aku Tenpa*, including the translated book *The Selection of Chinese Ancient Fables*. Otherwise I was involved in translations between Tibetan and Chinese literature, including some natural science and literary books, such as Agronomy and books about the Warring States Period, plus translating various fine Tibetan books into Chinese. This was a peak period for my academic translation. However, in the coming "fighting against the rightists" campaign and the "Cultural Revolution" in succession in 1966, I was profoundly and negatively affected and all my translation and research work had to stop.

In 1966, I returned to Kangding (Tardo in Tibetan). This injustice finally ended in 1978. In succession, I undertook the position of member of the standing committee of the Chinese People's Consultation Conference (CPPCC) of Garze Autonomous Prefecture, the deputy President of the Research Committee of Folk Arts Culture and Literature Federation of Garze, vice director of the Broadcasting Program Committee and member of the standing committee of the Ethnic Languages Committee of Sichuan. I was cited and rewarded as the provincial and prefecture-level model women entitled "the flag-carrying woman"...I returned completely to my teaching, research and editing. I held the post of Tibetan editor of the Journal *Mountain Gongkar* and teacher of the Ethnic Cadres' College of Garze Prefecture. Since the founding of the Tibetan night school in 1981 until 1991, over 400 students had graduated with Tibetan language and culture. In 1989, when I was 76 years old, I was granted the senior professional title of copy editor, and my academic status was formally recognized by the state.

The oral epic *King Gesar* is a treasure of Tibetan traditional culture. Therefore, I devoted my heart and mind to working on the rescue of the epic during the 1980s, including researching the different editions of *King Gesar*, translating and drafting a number of research papers to further the successful preservation of *King Gesar*. Because of my contributions, the State Ethnic Affairs Committee, the Culture Ministry, Chinese Culture and Literature Federation and the Chinese Academy of Social Sciences in 1986, cited me as an excellent individual. In 1997, I was again honored by the above-mentioned organizations.

Great Achievements

I have gone through my three peak periods of achievements throughout my life-long career. The first period was from 1943 to 1949 when I first experienced success in translation of Tibetan folk songs, proverbs and stories. I was particularly fond of Tibetan folk songs, and they were so marvelous and had such perfect rhythm. All of those Chinese translations were entitled *The Endless Stories* to be published respectively in the *Xinmin Evening Newspapers*, *Takungpao Newspapers* and *Zhong Yang Daily*. My virgin paper was entitled *Three Siblings Consulting a Fortune Teller*, which was published in the *Xinmin Evening Newspaper*. In 1947, I wrote a book entitled *Frontier of China*, in which I briefly described the natural geography and topography of Kham and its close relationship with the motherland. In this book, I particularly emphasized the significance of the development of the frontier of China. This book was fully supported by the senior governor of KMT government of the Republic of China and the governor authorized it for publication. I was a little bit famous during that period. Whenever I walked in the street, people wanted my autograph. I usually signed with the Tibetan words for "Blessings and Auspiciousness" on their books or notebooks. Since I came from Tibetan inhabited area, my complexion was often dark. The news media liked to refer me to as "the black peony fully equipped with beauty and a perfect voice". This was my first time to be on a board for translation and literary writing.

The second period of my success was from the early 1950s to the early 1960s, about 10 years. During this period, I kept on my path of working on translations of folk literature between Chinese and Tibetan. In succession. I published *Collection of Tibetan Folk Songs* (by cooperating with Tashi Tsering and published by Sichuan Ethnic Publishing Press in 1959) and *Stories of Aku Tenpa* (Published by Sichuan Ethnic Publishing Press in 1963). During this period, I began to translate Chinese literature into Tibetan, such as the books that I had myself, including 34 books of about 400 thousand characters each relating to natural sciences and social sciences. Apart from those on which I cooperated with Liu Jiaju and Kelzang, twelve publications appeared under my name. I became a fully-fledged translator during this period. On one occasion, a foreigner from the Czech Republic came to visit Sichuan Ethnic Publishing Press. When the visitor mentioned that his staff could translate 2000 words per day, the director of the Publishing Press said proudly: "Our Dondrup Lhamo is capable of translating 3000 words a day."

This was my second peak period in my career.

The third productive period of my career was during the 1980s and 1990s. When the "culture revolution" was over, I was entering my old age, but I was still full of energy and needed to do something. I told myself to recapture my lost time. I involved myself in the translation of a number of folk literary works, prose and the *Chinese-Tibetan Dictionary of Tibetan Medicine*. Other works included the *Proverbs of Sakya* (partial collection), Tibetan opera *Prince Drimed Kunden*, *Prince Norsang* and *The Coming Spring of Ethnic Languages*, *Singing the Old Soldier*, and *The Origin of Counties' Names in Garze and Their Historical Transformations*. I was rather outstanding and successful in the translation of and studies in the oral epic *King Gesar*. I translated *Song-Ling Battle* and *Salvation Of Mother from Hell*, a total of 130 thousands characters, in cooperation with Kelzang Chopahel as co-translators. Besides, I wrote up my research papers, such as *Outlining the Proverbs Of King Gesar's Legend*, *Outlining Drumo's Images Shown in King Gesar Legend*, *The Discussion on the Birth of King Gesar*, and so on. All of these have produced highly valued academic achievements and brought me favorable social outcomes. The Provincial Ethnic Affairs of Sichuan declared one of my papers an excellent research paper. This was the period when I reached the academic peak of my research.

In 1995, I transacted my retirement document. Even so, I never stop my working on Tibetan cultural preservation.

Issue: No.2, 2019.

16
THE CONCERNS OF A CENTURY-OLD GENIUS

— A Memory of Ngabo Ngawang Jigme from My Period of Working in Beijing

Text by Lhagpa Phuntshogs

On Dec. 23rd of 2009, Ngabo Ngawang Jigme, the great hero of the Tibetan people, close friend of the Communist Party of China and well-known social activist, left this world forever. This was a severe loss for the Tibetan people, the Communist Party of China and the state. Our sadness is overwhelming as we recalled our memories of this century-old genius.

I first met Ngabo Ngawang Jigme at Tibetan Public School, which was the origin of today's Tibetan Ethnic College in Xianyang. In 1959, as the deputy director of the Preparatory Committee of Tibet Autonomous Region, Ngabo Ngawang Jigme made a special inspection visit to the school. He gave an important speech in which he encouraged students to return to Tibet and participate in the democratic reform and reconstruction of their hometown. I was an 18-year-old student in a teachers' training class in the Tibetan Public School. Henceforth, I had several opportunities to meet Ngabo Ngawang Jigme and listen to his speeches while I also heard from various sources about his stories.

Due to the demands of my job and the location where I was working, I had few opportunities for direct contact with him. In May of 2000 after I began working in the China Tibetology Research Center in Beijing, I had more opportunities to learn from him. During this period, Ngabo Ngawang Jigme was already about ninety years old—a slim, white-haired man. Even so, his eyesight remained sharp and clear, in conjunction with a quick mind and eloquent speech. His concerns regarding Tibet, the Tibetan people, Tibetan culture and Tibetan studies were still extensive, sincere and ongoing. I would like to recount several instances in which I encountered Ngabo Ngawang Jigme over the years, expounding on his great concerns regarding Tibet.

His Heart Lies with the Motherland

My first meeting with Ngabo Ngawang Jigme after I transferred to Beijing was during the symposium to commemorate the 50th Anniversary of the Peaceful Liberation of Tibet held in the Great Hall of the People in 2001. In the symposium we listened to his important speech. I presented *khada* to Ngabo Ngawang Jigme and other central governors, and we took a group photo together. I recall that whenever there were activities related to any commemoration of the peaceful liberation of Tibet, the democratic reform of Tibet, any significant event occurring in Tibet or every moment the state council considered new approaches or strategies regarding Tibet, people could see him in person, hear his voice and read his papers and comments. His voice was clear; his attitude straight, his opinions precise and clear... which always impressed the mass of the people.

Recalling his congratulatory address to Tibet, he said: "As an old Tibetan who has experienced almost a century of drastic changes in Tibet, I sincerely wish I could celebrate all the historically meaningful moments and physically witness all the great changes taking place in my hometown during the decade. However due to my age and physical limitations, I couldn't pay a visit in person at this time to bring my congratulations, which I regret very much."

In a letter, he said: "The peaceful libration of Tibet, as matter of fact, is the wisest decision and greatest innovative undertaking during that particular historical period. This is a great achievement of the Communist Party of China in line with its principle of the equality and unity of nationalities in dealing with ethnic issues."

Taking Care of Tibetan Social Advancement

In early 2003, the leaders from the Economic and Trade Bureau of Lhasa Municipality of Tibet Autonomous Region and Lhasa Carpet Factory entrusted me to make an appointment with Ngabo Ngawang Jigme. They told me that, in early 1950s during the founding of Lhasa Carpet Factory, Ngabo Ngawang Jigme was the first president of the factory and while celebrating the 50th anniversary of the founding of this factory, they wished to report the changes in the factory to him and request his ongoing interest and support. I sent their solicitations to him through his secretary and Ngabo Ngawang Jigme agreed to meet us. Later, I accompanied the leaders of the factory and the committee to his residence. On seeing us, he was very happy and shook hands with us one by one. He listened patiently to their report and then repeatedly insisted on the importance of the smooth running of this factory. He said: "As a Tibetan traditional handcraft, the textile weaving technique of the carpet is one of the major components of Tibetan culture. To advance the Tibetan carpet industry will improve the income of the mass of Tibetans and boost employment while advancing the local Tibetan economy. Therefore, it is important to increase input, cultivate human resources and take a creative approach to new technology and new markets to fully exploit the market potential of this traditional industry." Afterwards, Ngabo Ngawang Jigme passed on the workers, opinions to the relevant departments of the local Tibetan government. They were highly appreciated and fully endorsed.

The reason Ngabo Ngawang Jigme cared so much about the issues of Tibetan social and economic development is because of his profound understanding of Tibetan society. In his paper written in 2009, he said:

"I was born in 1910, and I completely understand the Old Tibet before the democratic reform of 1959. Historically, Tibet was a theocratic feudal serfdom society that had lasted for a long period, with low levels of production and a desperate shortage of materials. The serf owners, composed of aristocrats, nobles and upper-class monks, accounted for less than 5 percent of the total population but possessed almost all the arable land, rangelands and most of the livestock. On the contrary the serfs, who accounted for 95 percent of the total population, not only had no rights over their own bodies, but also bore a heavy burden of land tax, taxation in various kinds and corvée labor, reducing them to poverty. The backward state of productivity and the remote geographical environment had caused Tibetan society to become isolated and conservative. The whole society was declining day by day. It was democratic reform that created a new epoch for Tibet, enabling Tibet to step into a new era with a new society. This approach not only liberated the serfs and the productivity of Tibet, but also saved Tibet as a whole."

Caring for the Preservation and Development of Ethnic Culture

On June 21st in 2004, the Celebration of the Founding of China Association for Preservation and Development of Tibetan Culture was held in the Great Hall of the People. Over 100 representatives interested in Tibetan culture and concerned for its preservation and protection attended this conference. Ngabo Ngawang Jigme was chosen as the president of the association. He happily accepted this offer and delivered an incandescent speech. He said that the founding of this association was a significant event, and it could attract more and more people to understand Tibetan culture and to care for its preservation and development. In addition, by taking advantage of this association, an ideal platform for presenting Tibetan culture to the world can be achieved. He believed that the ethnic Tibetan culture of China would surely bloom in the 21st Century and take its rightful place in the history of human civilization!

In the Tibetan New Year of 2004, the author (Left) visited Ngabo Ngawang Jigme. Photo by Wang Hong

As is well known, Tibetan traditional medicine is another key component of Tibetan culture. Ngabo Ngawang Jigme attached much importance and concern throughout his lifetime to the founding and development of Beijing Tibetan Hospital. As early as November 1992, he inscribed the words "Beijing Tibetan Hospital" on the hospital's plate in Tibetan script. In 2003 during the later stages of the SARS epidemic, he attended the ceremony of cooperative medical service between Beijing Tibetan Hospital and China-Japan Friendship Hospital. On March 20th of 2004, he wrote a petition to the National Development and Reform Commission to ask for continued support and care for the advancement of Tibetan traditional medicine and pharmacology. In his letter, he wrote: "With the care and support of the Central Government and the National Development and Reform Commission, the new buildings of Beijing Tibetan Hospital have been successfully completed and in use from 2003, creating another platform for the advancement of Tibetan medicine and pharmacology. Even so, Beijing

Tibetan Hospital is still facing some substantial difficulties in terms of a shortage of funds, medical equipment and infrastructure. Beijing Tibetan Hospital asks for further support from the state and approval regarding the second term project." This letter from Ngabo Ngawang Jigme caught the attention of the relevant state governmental department and soon brought a response.

Speaking of Tibetan traditional medicine and pharmacology, I actually came up with an interesting event. Ngabo Ngawang Jigme at 100 years old surely has the gift of longevity. Like most, I was very interested in his advice on how to have a long life. Therefore, I asked him directly. When he spoke of the experience of longevity, he commented that it was important to maintain a regular life while keeping the brain active. It is also crucial to exercise the hands and feet while eating properly including roughage such as *Tsampa* that can prevent diabetes. He usually took one tablet of "pearl seventy" (a Tibetan medicine) that he believed could not only treat but also prevent diseases. Soon he changed the topic to how to preserve and develop the elites of Tibetan traditional culture. He always wished that Tibetan medicine and pharmacology, which had emerged and developed in the Tibetan highlands throughout a long history, could make a contribution to all Chinese people (particularly regarding common human health problems). Benefiting from his instruction, I completed my book *Treasury of Health Care and Body Building—Tibetan Traditional Medicine*, which has been published by China Tibetology Publishing House in 2007. It amounts to the fulfillment of the wishes of Ngabo Ngawang Jigme.

Fostering the Prosperity and Development of Tibetan Studies

Since I transferred to China Tibetology Research Center in Beijing, our colleagues have developed a common feeling emerging from our daily practice in Tibetan studies. That is, the China Tibetology Research Center is shouldering a very significant responsibility to introduce Tibet, the Qinghai-Tibet Plateau, Tibetan culture and the status quo of Tibet to the world.

However, such an introduction could not be effective if only speeches and/or writing were applied... unless there was also some physical window of opportunity in which Tibetan culture could be physically seen and touched. Therefore, we brought our thoughts to Ngabo Ngawang Jigme, seeking his advice and support. After hearing our report, Ngabo Ngawang Jigme gave his full support to the plan of building a special platform in Beijing to introduce Tibetan culture in depth to the whole nation, as well as the world. He consequently forwarded our request to the Central Government. With his full support, the proposal to establish a Tibetan Cultural Museum was soon approved and the project launched. On his passing, the museum building has already stood firmly at a conspicuous location on the East Road of the northern 4th Ring in Beijing, and was ready to open to the public (Editor's note: on March 28th, 2010, it was opened). We believe it will not fail to live up to the vision of Ngabo Ngawang Jigme to showcase the charm and glory of contemporary Tibet.

The contribution of Ngabo Ngawang Jigme to the China Tibetology Research Center is almost impossible to adequately describe. During the founding ceremony for the China Tibetology Research Center, he expressed his heartfelt congratulations and happiness while addressing his earnest expectations. He inscribed the "China Tibetology Research Center", the journal *China Tibetology* and "The Bureau of Editing and Comparison Study in Tibetan Buddhist Canon" in Tibetan. He participated in many of the major activities of the China Tibetology Research Center, no matter whether run individually by China Tibetology Research Center or in cooperating with other organizations. One event that deeply impressed and touched us all was during the twentieth anniversary celebration of the founding of the Center on May 20th of 2006; he overcame the difficulties of age to pay a visit and have extensive and happy discussions with scholars. He participated in important activities and extended his profound congratulations. The then 97-year-old man left all present with a profound impression.

A Tibetan proverb says: "A standing pine can grow into an extensive forest." Ngabo Ngawang Jigme is just like this lofty pine standing firmly on the Qinghai-Tibet Plateau. Though he has left us, his spirit, ideology, character and moral strength will live eternally as if the moon, the sun and the evergreen pine, educating and encouraging us on our journey forever.

Issue: No.3, 2010.

17
THE FIRST FEMALE RADIO BROADCASTER DECHEN DRAMA

Text & Photo by Yang Enhong

Tibetans over the age of 60 or 70 may recall that 50 years ago, the news of peaceful liberation of Tibet was read by a female Tibetan radio broadcaster with a wonderful voice. During that time, there was no broadcast station in Tibet. The radio service was provided by the Southwest Broadcasting Station in Chongqing of Sichuan Province. Later, much important news was also broadcast by her. She was the first female Tibetan announcer in Tibetan history and whose name was Dechen Drama, a daughter from Gertse Dzong (the word Dzong in Tibetan corresponds to the word county) of Ngari in Tibet.

In the course of writing an oral history of Tibetan women, I was lucky to obtain an interview with Dechen Drama in Lhasa in the first half of August in 1996. She was a cheerful and easy-going lady. She had worked in various departments of the central government. When she was told the purpose of the interview, she talked about herself and her family without any hesitation.

Dechen Drama was born in 1930, and her zodiac sign was the horse. Her father passed away when she was one year old. Her brother Sonam Paljor inherited the official position of governor in Gertse Dzong in Ngari. Later she came to Lhasa where her family had some property.

The governor of Gertse Dzong in Ngari enjoyed great privileges in the nomadic area of Tibet because this governor was a fourth-rank officer. Whenever the third day of the Tibetan New Year came, her family was authorized to help the Dalai Lama to dress. Before the fifth Dalai Lama unified Tibet, all tribes administered their own lands separately. The pedigree of the governor of Gertse Dzong in Ngari belonged to the family of King Chongye in Lhoka. After the fifth Dalai Lama, the power of the governor of Gertse Dzong in Ngari did not change. During that time, if aristocrats wanted to have official positions they had to pay for them. However, the son of the governor of Gertse Dzong in Ngari could immediately inherit the position of governor at birth. Nevertheless, this position could only be granted to a boy (referred to as the "bone" of the lineage) but not a girl, even if the daughters of the family delivered the boy. Today the "bone" offspring of this family is only the man who may work in the local police station.

In the past, fourth-ranked officers were divided into interior and exterior fourth-rank governors. When meeting each other, these two officers did not necessarily have to dismount from their horses. When they met the Dalai Lama, they both could sit at the same level, and the only difference between them was their headgear. The interior governor could wear *Gavu*, but not the exterior one. The exterior governor's horse was decorated with only one red tassel when he headed towards Lhasa, but he was allowed to display either one or two red tassels on leaving Lhasa. In the old days, in winter, the governor of Gertse Dzong in Ngari must ask for leave directly from the Dalai Lama to return to Ngari from Lhasa. When summer came he had to return to Lhasa to report to the Dalai Lama and the four Kalons (Cabinet Ministers). The local Tibetan government had detailed regulations concerning procedures when the governor of Gertse Dzong in Ngari went out. That is, he was allowed to have eight retainers and nine horses (four in front and another four in the rear) while he rode in the middle in the procession). The governor of Gertse Dzong made annual cash payments to the Sera Monastery. He was not asked to pay any other taxes to the local Tibetan government. Apart from Gertse Dzong, the other Dzongs (counties) in Tibet were not authorized to implement their own criminal law but must make a formal request for approval from the local Tibetan government. Gertse Dzong, however, was different. It was empowered to enforce its own criminal law. In line with the regulations of the Old Tibet, men aged from 18 to 60 must serve in the army and no exception was allowed. However, this rule was not applied to the family of the governor of Gertse Dzong, and they were allowed to refuse such orders. In addition, before the fifth Dalai Lama, the governor of Gertse Dzong constantly enjoyed privileges that were referred to as "self-determining". He could go to India and Pakistan on business and even run shops on a simple request to the local government. During that period, Sikkim and Bhutan need to pay taxes not only to the local Tibetan government, but also to the governor of Gertse Dzong in Ngari.

The governor of Gertse Dzong enjoyed a high reputation not only in Ngari and Shigatse but also in Lhasa because of his considerable ability to run business. Up to the Cultural Revolution, people in Pakistan still sent money to the family because they had borrowed from the previous governor of Gertse Dzong. Because of such cases, Dechen Drama's brother, who was the son of the previous governor of Gertse Dzong, was charged with treason during the Cultural Revolution. The family had businesses not only in Dromo but also in some Indian cities and their goods could be transferred to Calcutta in India.

In Gertse Dzong, except for the family of the governor of Gertse Dzong, the populace was without houses. However, in the governor's family, the house had 100 pillars (the way in which Tibetans measure the size of their houses). These houses were later used as government offices for the Kangdor District of the government of Gertse County.

When Dechen Drama was about 10–11 years old, she was sent by her family to study in India. About half a year later, her mother was sick and she was asked to return to Lhasa. Since she had a wealthy family, she continued her studies in a private school in Lhasa.

In July 1950, Dechen Drama started work and was temporarily employed by the State Ethnic Affairs Commission. Later she worked in the Art Ensemble of the Southwest Army. In 1951, she participated in the war to resist US aggression in Korea. During that period, she joined the Youth League. As she had a wonderful natural voice the soldiers welcomed her songs during the war. At this time she started to learn Chinese. She had a pair of long pigtails that took her some time to comb so she was always late for military muster. Eventually she had no choice but to cut them off.

After returning to China from Korea, Dechen Drama was retained for service in the Southwest Military Force. She was an interpreter for the general-commanders of the military force, such as Chen Mingyi, Deng Xiaoping and He Long. Later she became a presenter for the Broadcasting Station of the Southwest Military Force. Dechen Drama, through the Southwest Broadcasting Station in Chongqing, broadcast the news about the peaceful liberation of Tibet and the death of Stalin. In 1952, the Southwest Administrative Committee was dismissed. Dechen Drama was transferred to the Central People's Broadcasting Station, serving in the International Department. During this period, she worked with some well-known broadcasters, such as Qi Yue (who was the team leader) and Xia Qing. In 1958, Dechen Drama was again transferred to work in the Tibetan Ethnic College in Xianyang.

During the appeasement of the armed rebellion in 1959, Dechen Drama educated her family members to support the Communist Party and rely on the People's Liberation Army (PLA). With her encouragement, her family members locked up all rifles and short-barreled guns. In the meanwhile, she encouraged the local monasteries in Gertse Dzong to lay down their arms to the PLA. Her brother Sonam Paljor, who was the governor of Gertse Dzong, died from high blood pressure on the way to a meeting in the government compound of Ngari. During that period, it is said that, two persons were the greatest contributors to appeasing the armed rebellion. One was Ngabo Ngawang Jigme, and the other was the governor of Gertse Dzong in Ngari. Because of the patriotic behaviour of the governor of Gertse Dzong and his

Dechen Drama (Right) with the anthor Yang Enhong.

family, the armed rioters particularly hated this family and robbed them of all of their property.

In 1962, Dechen Drama returned to Lhasa from Xianyang and worked in the Lhasa Broadcasting Station. During the Cultural Revolution, she was unfairly persecuted due to her family background. Despite the double whammy of these physical and spiritual ordeals, she kept working hard until retirement in 1992. Dechen Drama was once a member of the CPPCC Tibet Committee and enjoyed the county-level treatment.

In the autumn of 2006, I paid a visit to Dechen Drama in her house in Lhasa and presented her with the book entitled *Oral History of Tibetan Women*, which included her story. Dechen Drama is still a happy and optimistic person. She now has a joyful life with her family, bathing in the sunlight of the holy city of Lhasa.

Issue: No.3, 2010.

18
THE FRIENDSHIP BETWEEN MY FATHER AND THE LANGDUN FAMILY

Text by Lu Jibing

In 1952, my father, Xia Chuan, followed the march of the 18th Corps of the People's Liberation Army (PLA) into Tibet where he developed a deep friendship with the children of some noble families in Tibet.

After the entrance of the 18th Corps of the PLA into Tibet, the military force made its major task to unite the local government and people to implement the "17-article Agreement" and consolidate national defense. My father, while carrying out his task in the Information and Cultural Department, took charge of the Department of the United Front Work, from which his main task was to work with the former Silon (chief minister) Langdun Kunga Wangchuk and the Tibetan military commander Khemed Sonam Wangdu.

The Langdun family is also the family of the 13th Dalai Lama. On May fifth of 1876, the 13th Dalai Lama, Thubten Gyastso, was born into a rich farming family in Langdun Village close to Kongpo Gyamda to the east of Lhasa. On June 13th, 1879, the three-year-old soul boy became the 13th Dalai Lama, and soon the whole family was transferred to Lhasa where the Gaxag Government allocated them a large amount of land and houses. The father,

This is the 60-70 year-old building which was the one donated by Lungdun Kunga Wangchuk to the 18th Corps. During that period, the author's parents all worked in this building. Today it has become the car park area of the Political Department of the Tibetan Military Region Command. Corp as the office for the Political Department. It was used for a long time. This photo is the one the author shot in 2001 in Lhasa.

Langdun Kunga Rinchen, was appointed a Duke by the Empress Dowager and granted a ruby trapping. Since then, they became the first noble family in the modern history of Tibet. Even in 1940s the family possessed 15 manors, over 1000 serfs and 2000 head of cattle.

In Tibet, the aristocrats are categorized into three kinds. The first is Yabshi, i.e. the families of Dalai Lamas. There are only five of these families, and they are the "aristocrats of aristocrats". The Langdun family is listed as the first. The second is Depon, which is regarded as the most aristocratic family. Five of these families wielded all the authority and power of the regime before the peaceful liberation, as well as religious power. The remaining group is the other general aristocrats, accounting for about 200 families. These families had land and manors but mostly played no political role.

Langdun Kunga Wangchuk (1907–1981) is the nephew of the 13th Dalai Lama (his father, Langdun Dondrup Dorje, was the eldest child and thus qualified to inherit the position as Duke. The 13th Dalai Lama, according to his age, was ranked as the fourth amongst the other children.) After the death of the grandfather (Duke Langdun Kunga Rinchen) and his father, Langdun Kunga Wangchuk became the successor in the big family. At 14 years old, he worked for the Gaxag Government and in his 19th year he was promoted to the assistant of Silon Bonshod. In 1928, he formally became Silon (the official position of "Silon" is just next to "Kalon") and achieved a high level of authority and power in the Gaxag Government.

Langdun Kunga Wangchuk was a simple and honest person. After the signing of the "17-article agreement", he was one of the patriotic aristocrats who firmly supported the agreement.

Langdun Kunga Wangchuk also gave his full support to the 18th Corps of the PLA. When this Corps first arrived at Lhasa, there was no accommodation for the soldiers. He therefore agreed to allow the military to set up their tents in his manor and even gave them an empty family building to use as their office. To this day the eastern part of the Tibetan Military Area Command was originally part of the Langdun manor.

When the 18th Corps of the PLA marched into Tibet, Langdun Kunga Wangchuk's eldest daughter Pelmo was 17 years old, and his eldest son Paljor was 14 years old, they both had been studying in India. His another daughter, Tsering Drolkar, was 12 years old, and his son, Gonpo Tseten (7 years old), was a "Drapa" (Tibetan, meaning "common monk") in Lhasa. All his children usually wore elegant clothes and spoke very good English. They all exhibited simplicity and moderation.

At the very beginning, the communication between my father and the family members needed the assistance of a Tibetan cadre, Kalzang Yangang, to act as an interpreter. Later my father formed an acquaintance with them, found they could all speak English and he began to communicate with them in person by using English while applying a couple of Tibetan words he had just learned, but sometimes he had to use gestures. After a while, they began

Xia Chuan (Right 1) with Tsering Droma (Left1, 12 years old) and Gonpo Tseten (Middle, 7 years old) in 1952.

to understand each other without any problem and gradually developed a friendship.

Langdun Kunga Wangchuk and his wife, Tsering Wangmo, often invited my father to be family guests. In the peaceful courtyard with its luxuriant trees, they would sit together to talk about family matters, as well as national concerns. Whenever there were performances in Lhasa, the Langdun couples were invited to watch the performances together with other leaders, but their children always liked to sit with my father. When there was a movie show, the children preferred to go with my father as my father could translate for them in English.

Paljor wrote in his paper commemorating my father; "I had an over 50-year friendship with Xia Chuan. I can say positively and without any hesitation that we were all witnesses to the history of the peaceful liberation of Tibet."

"It was a sunny day in October of 1951. Xia Chuan arrived at Lhasa with the 18th Corps and lived in my family. At that time I was just 14 years old. I had a very clear memory of Xia Chuan who was wearing the military uniform. He was the director of the Department of Politics and Information of the 18th Corps of the PLA then. My parents called him 'Director Xia'. So we all called him that. Later his position was changed, but we found it difficult to change and still continued to call him 'Director Xia'."

"Director Xia and his military force were living with my family. He could not speak Tibetan and I didn't speak Chinese but both of us could speak a little bit of English. Therefore, English became our tool to communicate. He gave our family, and me, an important education by explaining the policy of the communist party. He told us the communist party was aiming to provide an overall service to the people and gain advantages for them. I learnt lots of new phrases and also a progressive ideology from him. Later, he asked me to get my education in Lhasa, as well as Mainland China. He said a rich knowledge could provide a better service to the Tibetan people. He liked to teach by precept and example. No matter how small the topic, he wanted to have an independent point of view. Through him, it was easy to see the fine quality and admirable spirit of the struggle by the PLA. There were so many things I learnt from him, which I could not get from books."

"I keep what director Xia told me deep in my heart. In Lhasa, I studied in a school run by the communist party and later had my further education in the Central University for Nationalities. After I graduated, I gradually learned how to write novels, poetry, commentaries and prose."

Frequent communication and getting along with each other formed a better understanding between people. It was just as a journalist said: "The democratic reform in 1959 not only liberated the slaves but also spiritually emancipated the aristocrats of Tibet."

In March of 1959, a handful of Tibetan separatists launched an armed rebellion. Langdun Kunga Wangchuk, together with his family, stood unfalteringly with the Tibetan people who did not run away from China by following the Dalai Lama, but rather remained as staunch patriots. In 1965 when the Tibet Autonomous Region was founded, he was elected vice-chairman for the government of the new autonomous region.

Langdun Kunga Wangchuk is good at Tibetan medicine and pharmacology, and he has produced a body of invaluable works. In his old age, he undertook several positions, including membership of the National Committee of CPPCC and vice-chairman of the CPPCC of Tibet Autonomous Region. He is an admired veteran patriot who gave his full support to maintain the unity of all the nationalities in China and fight against separatism.

He influenced his family members, even his relatives by marriage, Numa Migyur Dorje who was former regimental commander of the Tibetan military force residing in Shigatse. In 1955, the Ministry of National Defense promoted him to Lieutenant Colonel. In the armed rebellion of 1959, most of the army officers joined the rebellion, but he did not. He stayed in the country and took the positions of director of the Education and Cultural Bureau of Lhasa Municipality and deputy director of the Bureau of Education and Culture of Tibet Autonomous Region.

After the democratic reform, Langdun Kunga Wangchuk's children were all working in government departments. His eldest daughter, Pelmo, was the deputy director of the Tibetan Opera Group, and his son-in-law Wangdu was a famous photographer. His eldest son, Paljor, took the positions of Deputy Director of the Bureau of Broadcasting and TV of Tibet Autonomous Region, deputy to the National Congress and member of the standing committee of the CPPCC. Currently he is the vice chairman of the Tibetan Association of Writers.

In 1955, my father was transferred to Beijing, but he still maintained communication with the Langdun family. Whenever Lungdun Kunga Wangchuk came to Beijing for a meeting, he would always come to visit my family. His several children got their education in the Central University for Nationalities and frequently received help from my father. In the late 1970s, his granddaughter Pegyi (about 11–12 years old) studied in the Beijing Dance

In 2005, the author was invited to Lhasa and paid a special visit to Paljor's family, including Tsering Droma (Right 2), young brother Gonpa Tseten (Left 2) and his son, Norbu Tsering (Right 1).

School. She became a member of my family by coming to visit us every weekend with her Tibetan classmate, Droma.

In that year I was studying at the Tank School in Beijing and went home every weekend. So I often took her as my little sister to tour Beijing where I took photos for her. Currently she is a famous dancer in Tibet.

In 1981, my father was again transferred to work for the Tibetan Military Region and returned to Lhasa. The day after he arrived in Lhasa, his first visit was to the wife of Langdun Kunga Wangchuk, since her husband had already passed away, and also other old friends; Gya Sholpa, Sholkhang and Tupten Danda. On my father's second visit to Tibet he founded the Tibetan Cultural and Literature Association. He was concerned for the development of Tibetan culture and literature, holding forums and meetings regarding its development. This was a glorious moment in the advancement of Tibetan culture and literature.

In 1983, my father retired. Though he did not return to Lhasa again, he never cut his connection with his Tibetan friends, particularly the several children from the Langdun family.

In 1991, Paljor and his wife came to Beijing and stayed with our family for a long time. Though he was usually a taciturn person, whenever he was with us he was never silent.

One day in March 1992, my father suddenly received a letter from one of the daughters, Tsering Droma. She reminded us of the family connection by saying: "Whenever my family mentioned you, everybody felt so happy because your name took us back to the time when the 18th Corps of the PLA was stationed in Tibet. During that particular period, you often brought happiness and friendship to everyone in our family..." On reading such a letter, my father dissolved into tears and his memory was filled by many stories from that particular period.

My father passed away in 2005. That coincided with the 40th anniversary of the founding of Tibet Autonomous Region. My younger brother and I, on behalf of my father, took part in the celebration in Lhasa, where we also paid a special visit to Paljor and his family, including his younger sister Tsering Droma, younger brother Gonpo Tsering and his son Norbu Tsering.

At present, we have already seen the fifth and sixth generations of the Langdun Family. In the fifth generation, apart from Pegyi the famous dancer and vice chairman of the Tibetan Association of Dancers, the son of Gonpo Tsering, Norbu Tsering, is a well-known writer.

Paljor remembered: "Director Xia entered Tibet in 1951, and in 1955 he was transferred to the Ba Yi (Aug. 1st) Film Studio as the vice president. Once he returned to Beijing, he visited the Central University for Nationalities to see me and encourage me to study hard. He educated me to be independent and strong. I remember his words until today."

"In 1981, Director Xia was sent to Tibet again. The next day after his arrival he paid a visit to my family. He cared about everybody in my family. He said: 'I am your relative so our friendship surpasses any general friendship!'"

"After he came to Tibet he was appointed a member of the standing committee of the Communist Party of TAR, deputy political commissar of the Tibetan Military Region Command and honorary chairman of the Tibetan Cultural and Literary Association. He became more stringent towards me, asking me to write more and better quality works. With his encouragement my writing began to blossom with real achievements, including 'The Turmoil of Gardens', 'Decoration of Turquoise' and 'The Spring of the Eulogy'. My many novels, prose writings and poems have won national awards and some of them have been selected as prescribed texts for middle schools."

"The friendship between director Xia and me is intimate but not over-familiar. It is a pure friendship. When he worked in Lhasa, I did not ask him to help in private affairs. On the other hand, he never came to bother us. Whenever I went to Beijing for a meeting, I always paid him a visit and he received me kindly and hospitably. He treated us as his relatives. He often sought information from us about the changes and living standards of local civilians. In particular, he was especially interested in the development and construction of Tibet. Whenever he heard of the substantial changes taking place in Tibet, he was always very excited. "

"I, in return, also believed he was my relative and the connection between him and our Tibetan people is stronger than the Yarlung Zangpo River and deeper than the Yamdrok Lake."

Issue: No.4, 2011.

19
YANGJEN, THE FIRST TIBETAN FEMALE LAWYER

Interviewee: Yangjen, President of Heng Feng Law Firm
Interviewed and transcribed by: Chen Benjian
Location: The Sunny City of Lhasa Municipality
Date: September 8th, 2010

In Lhasa, many people call Yangjen "Big Lawyer".

As the first group of Tibetan lawyers in Tibet and actually the first female lawyer, the first lawyer to open a collective law firm in Tibet and the first individual to open a private law consultation firm, Yangjen holds many "first" in Tibetan law.

Why has she been so innovative? Yangjen replied firmly: "I am always confident in myself."

Perhaps I should start with a story about my childhood. At five years old I moved to Lhasa with my parents because their job position had changed. It was in this city that I completed my education from primary school to senior middle school. In middle school I was really good at sport. My short-distance running and high jump were outstanding. Many people suggested I should develop my sporting skills to pursue a professional sporting career but I chose to be a lawyer.

In 1981, I graduated from senior middle school and was enrolled in the Law Department of the Southwest Politics and Law University. I was one of five Tibetan students enrolled by this university in that year. The motivation to study law at that time was very simple, judicial and law-related jobs had high status since uniforms were given to staff. As a senior middle-school student, I had no idea about law or what role it played in society. I even had no idea about why I should study law, what it would do for my career and what role I must play in the practice of law. I was completely unconcerned about it and had no ambitions at all.

Of course, my primary choice, to some extent, was influenced by my parents. My parents came from Chamdo. During the democratic reform they were sent to Tibet College for Nationalities in Xianyang of Shanxi Province for their education and soon they had a job. Perhaps it was at that time they developed their great ambition for a prestigious job in law.

When I studied in Lhasa Middle School, I never thought about the differences between ethnic Tibetan and ethnic Han. On entering university, the change in circumstance first made me aware that I was a minority. The university was in Chongqing where there were few ethnic students. There were only five in my year. In the whole university there were only 20 Tibetan students. In addition to the number of ethnic students being small, their learning capacity was weaker than that of Han students. The entrance score for university was usually about 500–600 points, but we ethnics only managed 300 points, almost a half lower. At the beginning I felt under great pressure and spent all my time studying diligently. It was a difficult life for students before taking the national entrance examination for universities but after they were enrolled in a university, they could relax a little bit. However, in complete contrast, we Tibetan students put in more effort to catch up with the other students by taking extra study. Fortunately, due to my efforts, my first-year semester examinations were satisfactory, ranking ahead of my classmates. In my final semesters, I was chosen as the study representative of the class. I joined the Communist Party of China during my university years.

I graduated in 1985. There was time left for me to choose to either

Yangjen. Photo by Wang Shu

continue my education or pursue a career. Two of my classmates chose to go to Beijing for further education but I decided to return to Tibet to begin my career. At that moment I remembered that my family and university had told me it was always this way, people should return to their origins to make their contribution to society after university.

I was assigned to work in the Administrative Department of Notarization and Lawyers of the Judicial Bureau of Tibet Autonomous Region. This department is divided into two sections: one for administration of notarization and the other for administration of lawyers. However, basically there were no lawyers in Tibet, let alone law institutes. In the early 1980s, the national judiciary system had just been restored. When I was completing my internship, many places in China only had law consultation offices.

Frankly speaking, at that time I already had a comfortable job in the administrative area that was quite a satisfying career. The odd thing was there were no law institutes and lawyers in Tibet. So the question was, who I was going to administrate? In addition, the national judiciary examination system did not exist during that time.

I graduated in July 1985. In October of the same year, the first law service institute was founded in Tibet: the Lhasa Law Consultation Center. My classmates and several others, who had graduated earlier, worked as part-time lawyers. It was then that I started my law career.

At that moment, I did not realize I had such potential in law. Progressively, the more I worked at it the more I liked it very much. A career as a lawyer is in fact a challenging profession. It requires strong capacity for independence while working. Whenever I started on a new case, I had to independently think it over and come up with a firm decision by myself. It is good to discuss with colleagues and get their suggestion, but sometimes they are very busy and then you have to work on your own. Nonetheless, if you can completely apply your knowledge in court, if your suggestion is adopted, if you are flexible and can cope with the vagaries of law, if your wisdom gains recognition by judges and prosecutors, if your responsibility and accountability are recognized by clients and trusted by juries… it is an absolutely fascinating profession. This feeling has nothing to do with money. Those cases we worked on did not in fact make any profits.

I recall that when I worked on my first case, I held the documents but never thought to discuss it with anybody. During that period, my bosses did not understand law and I had to come up with my own ideas. Before court opened, I made a comprehensive preparation. I read all the documents and tried hard to find evidence, but when court started I could not read my statement fluently. My legs shook. On returning home I told my family that I doubted I was capable of doing this job. My mother encouraged me by saying: "You must be persistent in everything. If you do not keep on trying, how do you know whether you could succeed or not?"

That was a robbery case which it was rather complicated. Four farmers in Lhundrup County sold a water pump placed on a farm. In the first trial it was determined to be robbery and the farmers were sentenced to five to nine years' imprisonment respectively. The water pump was originally purchased for about 4,000 Yuan. The court issued a sentence based on the price on the invoice for purchasing this machine. In the 1980s, such a large amount of money was something to be taken seriously. On receiving this case, I carefully read the documents and found it was not mentioned when the water pump was bought. According to the four defendants, the water pump had not been used for many years so that they guessed it had been discarded. Therefore, they decided to take it away to sell it as scrap iron. I found that the owner of the water pump had purchased it over ten years and it was actually damaged two years ago. Evidence showed the pump had been write-off and its value must include depreciation due to its age, not the original price. Therefore, the water pump must be taken to Lhasa for appraisal. From Lhundrup to Lhasa usually takes two hours by car since the road is rough. I used a tractor to get that pump back to Lhasa. The professional appraisal concluded the water pump was useless. With such evidence in the second trial, these four farmers were determined to be "not guilty".

On hearing this result, the relatives of the four defendants became very excited and relieved from the pressure of the first trial. I was so proud to observe their appreciation and excitement. My efforts were recognized by the fact that the previous sentence was over-turned. At the start of my career in law, I experienced success by applying my knowledge to help people achieve justice. I was encouraged and recalled that the team in law service at that time was not professional since staff had been transferred from different organizations without any professional training in law. Though I only learned theory in school, I was the only professional person on the team.

Later, the four farmers often came to visit me bringing eggs and butter that I could not refuse. I know this is the way they show their appreciation. To these civilians having a lawsuit is a big issue. If unfortunately, the court had sentenced them to seven to eight years, the rest of their lives would have been completely changed. In addition the four families, their children and parents, would have been negatively affected.

These days I often instruct younger lawyers to treat all cases carefully and seriously. This is the fundamental principle behind being professional. As lawyers, we face lawsuits everyday. Some may be big and others may be small. Any of our cases is just one amongst a large number of lawsuits. However, to the clients this is a major event in their lives. Therefore, any one of my cases, no matter whether it is a small case involving several thousand yuan or big involvement of money, I always treat it seriously and carefully.

Due to the small number of lawyers in Tibet (about 100 lawyers in total) I have to at least be present in court three to four times weekly. Almost every day I am fully occupied. During the day I investigate my cases and at night I prepare my documents. I almost never get any leisure time but just keep busy day and night. Quite often, when I come back home, I am extremely tired and do not want to talk.

In the beginning of the 1990s, the state launched a reform of legal institutions and encouraged lawyers to work independently from the institutes. At this time, as a lawyer I had already practiced for seven to eight years in which time I had accumulated some experience. I therefore wanted to see if I could survive independently. In 1993, I left my post in the state-run organization and funded the first collective law firm. I was president of this firm. Before I joined this law firm, I was affiliated with the Bureau of Judiciary of Tibet Autonomous Region. My salary was provided by the state. I was actually 29 years old at that time.

To a lawyer, running a business in a private firm is rather different from working in government organizations. On leaving government organizations, we have to be more self-reliant. We can act while resting entirely on our own judgment. Nevertheless, without great individual capacity, it is hard to survive. In addition, without courage and hard work, it is also hard to keep on going. Moreover, responsibility and accountability, working together with complete records, are all the indicators needed to help you survive.

Only four to five years afterwards did my family know that I had left government post. At that time, I also convinced my younger brother to give up a government post to work with me as lawyer. He had graduated from Beijing Youth Political College and afterwards he worked for the Youth League of Tibet Autonomous Region. He studied law in his university.

Since the first day I became a lawyer, I have never stopped working hard. I worked even harder after leaving my government post. I almost never had a holiday or a weekend. I tried my best to take every case and accumulate experience, resulting in a good reputation in society. People learned about my law firm through my cases and gradually they knew me. We soon had a good standing in society. Frankly speaking, I was quite successful. My salary during that time was 460 yuan, which was rather high for that particular period.

My younger brother, Chophel, is a brilliant person. From 1992, he has worked with me until today. During this time, he has spent four years studying law in the United States. In 2005, after he came back from the United States, he suggested to me that we offer public welfare assistance and not only serve those clients who could pay but also to provide a service to those who could not afford to pay. He believed that although working in our firm was strenuous, we had a satisfactory income. Therefore, we should accept some social responsibility.

In 2006, with the approval of the Bureau of Judiciary of Tibet Autonomous Region, we registered the Yangjen Law Support Center of Tibet. This was the first private law support center in Tibet. In the past, we took on some legal support work, but did not have any specific institution and of course did not issue any publicity in this regard. Nowadays, the formal establishment of the law support center must be taken seriously in line with regulations.

At Gonggar Airport, we now have a big advertising billboard on which we inform the public of our public service activities, address and telephone number. We would like to advertise extensively to the public to tell them how we could give them help through the law. Amongst all the various kinds of business advertisements displayed in the airport, only ours is a public welfare advertisement.

We offer consultations through a hot line service and face-to-face communication in order to provide all kinds of service to locals while organizing lawyers to provide a voluntary service.

We rented a place close to the Tibetan library to run a Law Library and we raised the capital to purchase over 6,000 books so that people could come there to research into the law.

Along with the advancement of the Tibetan economy and resulting social development, there are many outside laborers being attracted by this development. However, they often face some infringement situation such as a delay in payment or a dispute over an industrial injury. In addition, the number of Tibetan farmers and herdsmen who come to urban areas to sell their labor is increasing. Consequently, we are receiving an increasing number of cases from them year by year. Amongst all cases regarding the labor of people from rural areas, Tibetans represent almost one fourth. In the past, Tibetans did not like to labor outside their village, but rather preferred to stay with their family to cultivate the land. Keeping abreast with social advancement, their attitude has changed dramatically. In particular many young people want to seek employment outside their hometown. Nonetheless, their salaries are low because of their lack of skills on one hand and the lack of safeguards of their rights on the other. Many Tibetan workers are satisfied with their situation. They believe it is enough to have a basic income instead having nothing. However, from the perspective of fairness, some enterprises do discriminate against them. For instance, for the same laboring work like carrying sand and bricks, they can receive different rates of payment.

Speaking of the rights of the laborers from rural areas, in 2007, we formed a workstation especially to deal with the lawsuits of farmers and herdsmen attempting to safeguard their legal rights. This workstation is affiliated with the law support center. Concerning labor disputes, the most people want to seek help from the laboring and human-resource departments in order to obtain arbitration. Therefore, we hung our advertisement billboard at the entrance of the arbitration committee. We included the address and telephone number of our workstation so that people can easily get access to us. Additionally, whenever rural laborers visit the arbitration committee, they are advised to come to us since the cost of a lawyer from the society is very expensive and they usually cannot afford it.

Since the establishment of the workstation, we have obtained support from the government judiciary and the national lawyer association. Through projects, they have granted us 200,000 yuan annually. We usually cover the extra costs.

In 2009, we founded the Tibetan Fund for Law Support to explore as many channels as possible to fund law support activities on the one hand, and to offer an opportunity for lawyers in Tibet to help society and to be responsibility to society on the other. At present, the Fund is just in its early stages but some institutions and enterprises have expressed their interest in offering support already.

In recent years, we have contributed a lot to the public welfare law service, in terms of time and energy, and in particular we undertake a lot of work in regard to organizing, administering and management. I personally undertake all the work involved with lawsuits, training lawyers and coordinating with outsiders. After all, I know many people and many people in the society know me. Given my younger brother and I are so successful, my younger sister is a little interested in our cause. She is really good at English and is working in the international department of the Post Office. She commented that if she retired, she would like to join us in the law support center.

Nowadays our firm has a staff of over 20 people plus some interns and part-time lawyers. When they get some free time, they come to the center to provide a service for some amount of income. Besides I undertake the position as deputy Chairman of the Lawyers' Association of Tibet Autonomous Region. Whenever the association holds meetings, I like to give "tasks" to those who come from different prefectures of Tibet by telling them that if they have few cases in a year, they could receive cases under the name of the Law Support Center, and then at the end of a year, they could bring these cases to the center to receive reimbursement of their costs. Generally, we pay every individual case about 1,500 yuan.

In order to enhance the quality of the lawsuits we receive, we run a training program for lawyers and volunteers. Right now we have already run four terms of professional training program under the sponsorship of the Bureau of Commence and Trade of Tibet Autonomous Region.

Since the founding of Yangjen Law Support Center, it has received great support from different levels of society. Successively, the Ministry of Judiciary and Law cited us as "National Excellent Team on the Performance of Law Support" and "National Excellent Team to Provide a Creative Service, Promote and Maintain a Harmonious Society".

On recalling my 25-year career as a lawyer, I must say I am proud of what I have done. The Heng Feng Law Firm consists of a well-performing team. In these years, we have received over 3,000 cases. About 80 percent of our comments during lawsuits are adopted in court. 160 enterprises and collective units have invited us to be law consultants. Our efforts helped us recover an economic loss of about one hundred million yuan for these entities. I was also invited to be the law consultant for the government of Lhasa Municipality. I participated in many complicated lawsuits including some economic cooperation surveys, negotiations, drafting of contracts and dealing with dispute cases. My contribution has won the recognition of the society and I was successively cited as "one of the national excellent lawyers", "model individual of the nation to promote law education", "one of the ten national outstanding youth", "the female vanguard holding the red flag in Tibet Autonomous Region" and "one of the ten outstanding youth of Tibet Autonomous Region".

As one of the first group of lawyers in Tibet, I dare to say I am a witness of Tibet. The history of my career reflects the progress of the law in Tibet.

The Ethnic Tibetan, frankly speaking, has no awareness of law throughout past history. Whenever encountering disputes and conflicts, our people usually seek help from either relatives or friends, senior people from their community or sometimes Rinpochers from monasteries to give arbitration. Needless to say on going to court for a dispute, people feel embarrassed to consult law firms. They would rather consulate us secretly but not publicly by inviting us their home. They believe any lawsuits could bring loss of face in public. People always think in this way, no matter if they are plaintiff or defendant.

Therefore, when I started my career as a lawyer, I took on many criminal cases. In parallel with the advancement of the society, the common people have increased their awareness of law. Beginning from the early 1990s, the increasing number of civil lawsuits and economic lawsuits drives them to seek help through the law.

In addition, enterprises also started to have more awareness of law, in particular when they realize the advantage of economic contracts. In the past, our Tibetans abstained from contracts, as they believe "contracts" symbolize distrust. They believe cooperation between people must be based on mutual trust. Otherwise there is no meaning in cooperation. Oral commitment is the fundamental negotiation between business partners. At present, no matter whether big enterprises or small workshops, they have fundamentally changed their ideology. Many enterprises employ permanent law consultants. In our firm, many lawyers have signed contracts with them as permanent law consultants. Whenever these enterprises encounter conflict and disputes, they come to research law related matters, including business negotiations, drafting contracts, amending contracts and so on.

As a lawyer for many years, people often ask me which lawsuit was my best performance. I reply by saying this was actually a difficult question to answer because there is no standard that can be used to measure. I won success in my work, including helping many people avoid jail sentences and retrieving economic losses. Also, many disputes were finally solved because of my efforts to make both sides shake hands to make up. In all my cases I drove myself to work hard. My heart always went with anyone involved in my cases. Judges admired my input into every individual case, and I actually treated all cases as my own family issues and was determined to solve them.

Nowadays there are many lawsuits, particularly in economic cases. Usually clients want to maximize their profits. They often hold unreasonable desires and sometimes their wishes are beyond the capacity of laws and regulation. At this moment, as lawyers, we must end their dreams by informing them what is rational and what the law does not support. We must also tell them as their lawyers that we will definitely maintain their rights in any way, but this must be based on following the principals of the law to be fair and just. There is no room to do anything that should not be allowed by law. Otherwise, notwithstanding how good a lawyer is in debate, law is the only principle applying in court. As lawyers, we must be ready for every assessment.

Objectively speaking, in my every debate in court, I do a good job. I am recognized as a lawyer with quick reactions, eloquent language and smart performance in practice. I always produce some surprises for my clients by presenting the court with different thoughts. My clients acknowledge my flexibility in court.

My clients are cheerful when I win their cases. So am I. Nonetheless, the loser in court often hates me at that particular moment. Fortunately, sooner or later they recognize I am a lawyer who has tried my best to be responsible and accountable, capable and fair. Finally, some of them come to me years later to ask for my help when they become involved with other lawsuits or sometimes they come to seek a consultation in disputes.

As a result of the satisfaction of clients and also the recognition of the opposite point of view, I believe this is the way to success.

In fact, most work is done outside the court, especially in economic disputes. We usually make a tremendous effort to mediate in order to make a compromise possible.

I often tell my clients to have perspective. I said: "If you could make a compromise with the opposite view, you may not gain all of what you expect, but your honesty will make it possible for your opponent to recognize your loss and in turn it maybe make it somehow possible for both sides to reach some cooperation. On reaching some cooperation, both sides may later achieve much more success and be more profitable. For instance, one of my clients is an enterprise that always had trouble cooperating with other enterprises during their two to three years' of cooperation. Finally they had a dispute and came to me for mediation. I sincerely told them to look forward and not to take small issues so seriously in business. With my comments, they compromised with each other and decided to continue the cooperation for four to five years.

"If it is possible to walk one step back, do it." These are words I often say and this is my personal principle as a human being.

As a lawyer, I must understand I am human, which means I must have sympathetic feelings for people. For instance, regarding cases such as a delay in payment for construction projects, no payment at all or having no ability to pay legal fees… I like to give them special treatment. Encountering such a situation, some lawyers do not like to receive these cases or may contribute less in court. I am against such a way of dealing with these cases and I will suggest they could pay me later, but I never treat the case carelessly. On the contrary, I contribute all of my energy to do my best. I think this is the mark of being professional and how to be human, just like a doctor who could not neglect his/her patient due to lack of money to pay the bill.

I enjoy talking about my cases. Sometimes I even forgot to talk about the fee when clients first come to me. After the close of lawsuits, my clients come to me to express their appreciation and some come to offer more money for my excellent performance which brought about their final success. Of course, I also meet people who paid me little or nothing even though I won the case for them.

Whenever encountering clients who have a very bad economic situation or sometimes the case is prolonged, I usually not only help them to continue the lawsuits but also sponsor them for some of their costs for accommodation and transport. Many people comment I am an easy-going person.

My ethnic Tibetan people are accustomed to the tradition of helping others. We always like to help people without any expectation to get payback. My thought may be influenced by my people. I would like to do whatever I can to help others.

Issue: No.5, 2011.

20

SINGING SOUNDLY WITH GRATITUDE

Text & Photo by Li Hui

Before seeing Asgen I had imagined a girl who has been on the stage of various parties on CCTV (China Central Television) many times for such a young age. She might have the air of a star but when I saw her the first time, my former suspicions all vanished right away. Before me, was a Tibetan girl who is so pretty, nice and easy going.

When Asgen did the interview with me, the sunshine shone through the window and it was warm and peaceful in the room. As she spoke to me, her eyes were attentive and her voice seemed to penetrate one's heart with enchantment.

Out of the Mountains for Her Beloved Singing

Asgen was born in the Aba Tibetan-Qiang Autonomous Prefecture, Sichuan Province. The scenic mountains and waters in Sichuan bring Asgen up to be a pretty girl. The secret and solemn snowy highland gives Asgen a voice as broad and clean as a prairie. "Asgen" means "auspicious glory of Buddha" in Tibetan. Asgen's parents might have hoped that fortune and auspiciousness would surround their daughter forever. As they had expected, Asgen's life is really full of auspiciousness and luck.

Asgen is singing in Tibet.

Asgen grew up in a simple environment of singing and dancing, so she inherited the skill of Tibetan people at song and dance. She said: "I have loved singing since I was little. My family support me, especially my grandma. I have a good voice and some local fame. I was encouraged to pursue the road of music." Because of her wonderful voice, she was often asked to give shows when she was in primary and junior high school. Later, she applied for a major school of vocal music under the advice of her family upon her graduation from the senor high school. At that time, Asgen didn't know that vocal musicians have to be trained by professionals; neither did she know that she should find someone to teach her. "I was lucky. The Central University for Nationalities admitted me because of my original singing.

During the college study, my teachers didn't dismiss my method. Instead, they taught me according to my merits and added scientific techniques to my original singing so as to enhance my music base. Now when I recall the past, the original singing might be my trait." Entering the Central University for Nationalities made it possible for Asgen to escape her former, isolated small town to the big stage of Beijing. Then, when she was enrolled into the Art Troupe of the Political Department of the Air Force, Asgen began to transform from a little girl who loved singing to a bright, Tibetan singer.

Sing Passionately to Bless Good Fortune

Asgen has always striven to make progress since she joined the Art Troupe of the Political Department of Air Force. Every year she follows the troupe to convey gratitude to the grass roots army, presenting her wonderful singing to the soldiers in the basic military units. For three successive years, she has been specially invited to take part in the "Beijing New Year's Concert" held in the People's Great Hall. The haunting rhythms of Tibetan music always capture the audience's hearts. As the first Tibetan singer to sing in the National Theatre, she has participated in the performance of the opera *Sister Jiang*. Being a messenger helping pass on the plateau culture, she has followed the state leaders to visit a dozen of countries and regions.

The most distinguished achievement is that she opened her personal solo concert, "*Mt. Qomolangma · Snow Lotus*", in Baoli Theatre during the both Anniversary of National Day and also the sixtieth anniversary of the establishment of our Air Force. To celebrate the birthday of our country and our air force, Asgen performed a number of sweet songs in her loud and broad voice in Tibetan costume at the concert.

Asgen said: "As a young Tibetan singer, it is a challenge for me to sing so many songs of different nationalities and styles. In addition, there is a lot to do for a concert, including costumes, props, and so on. I had to do everything by myself. So I went through an anxious time while I was busy with my concert. For me, it was a hard time. Fortunately, I succeeded in getting it done. Now when I recall it, I feel that the first thing I want to say is thanks: first to give thanks for the good times that gave me the opportunity to stand on the stage singing the best songs from my heart, and express the passionate patriotism of Tibetan people in the form of a concert." With these words, Asgen gave a smile of pride, her eyes shining and sparkling.

Praise for the Times with Lyrics

The inspiration from the concert planted another seed of hope in Asgen's heart: to enable more and more people hear her voice, experience the charm of Tibetan music and get to know the happy life of the Tibetan people. After a long preparation, Asgen's first solo album, *How Far is it to Get to Lhasa*, was released to face the world in 2010. "The production team is very professional, gathering many important figures who I respect much in the contemporary domestic music circle, such as Yan Su, Zhang Qianyi, Yin Qing, Meng Qingyun and Lei Yuansheng.

The album has thirteen songs of different styles, such as *How Far is it to Get to Lhasa, Heart of Fragrance, China—My Dear Mother*... every song is so beautiful in its lyrics and rhythm. When I sing them, images from the Tibetan areas seem to appear before my eyes, as if I had returned to my beloved hometown." Especially the theme song, *How Far is it to Get to Lhasa*, is also the theme music for the movie *The Qinghai-Tibet Railway*, directed by the famous director Feng Xiaoning and also one of the best works created by Zhang Qianyi in recent years after his other songs, *The Qinghai-Tibet Plateau, Enter Tibet, On the Peak of East Mountain*. Asgen expresses that song perfectly in her special and graceful voice, presenting a scroll of spiritual paintings containing the essence of her culture.

When we talked about the album, Asgen seemed to become a chatterbox, from which I could see that she loved her record very much. "I want to make more people understand how pure and holy Tibetan music is, and to let everyone feel kinship with the big national family." If you listen to her, you can detect her enthusiasm and gratitude for the people and the world.

"More and more youngsters are getting to like Tibet, the art and culture of Tibet...and especially Tibetan music. The national art shall be globally acknowledged. As a Tibetan daughter, I have to try my best to do anything related to my nationality well, to tell the world about our fine and happy life." Upon these words, Asgen grew attentive and serious.

Pay Back Society with Gratitude

In her life of more than twenty years, Asgen has been endowed with luck and happiness. That's why she is always grateful for all she has achieved. In her heart, to participate in various public charities is the most important thing except for her singing career. These days, Asgen subsidizes students in her hometown in order to let more children have the opportunities to get to know the outside world and to go out for further study. She also went to see the aged at the Seniors' Homes both in Beijing and the suburbs, giving shows for them; She took part in the benefit performance for victims of the earthquake which was held in Wenchuan of Sichuan and Yushu of Qinghai. She is enthusiastic about charitable causes, and would like to help those who are in need with all her efforts from singing songs in various benefit events.

This young Tibetan girl has a lot "titles": member of China National Minority Vocal Music Association, member of the Youth League of Central State Organs, member of the Youth League of Sichuan Province, and so on. In 2010, she was assigned membership of China Association for Preservation and Development of Tibetan Culture. In her eyes, to be worthy of all these honours awarded by the state and party, she has to try her best to do what she can. She said: "Since my country and party give me so many honors, I have to shoulder the mission behind them, to better inherit and spread the excellent Tibetan music and culture, because I believe that national art should be globally acknowledged. I will also devote all my efforts and energy to do the music I like, to develop all sides of the art. Otherwise, I feel I am disgracing my country and party unless I foster and favour them, and deserve my people's love for me.

During the interview, what Asgen said most is “good luck and thank you”. It is true that Asgen is fortunate. She is an eyas rushing into the shrine of art and ready to fly high with her wings. Han Hong, Assistant Chief of the Art Troupe of the Political Department of the Air Force, was full of praise when she talked of Asgen: “Gold will shine sooner or later just as the glory of highland’s glory goes through the clouds and mist.” Asgen’s success stems from her affection for both the music and the snowy highland. She has been awarded the second medal for singing in the 3rd National Minorities Art Festival of Sichuan Province, first medal for performance in the National College Art Festival, Honourable Mention in the professional group of the 6th National Military MTV Competition. Behind this accumulation of honours is a history of painstaking effort, which helps Asgen to progress further and further along the road of art.

Issue: No.5, 2012.

21
LOSANG

Text & Photo by Jigme Phungyel

Losang is 78 years old and is known as the God of longevities.

Losang is now 78 years old, one of the villagers who enjoy longevity. He is the former villager head of Dangram Village, also a senior Party member. By right of his senior experience, he is really somebody of the village.

It was Losang who sent us to Dangram in earlier times and provided horses and mules for us as we went around the local families. In those days, we had two women members who had never ridden a mule before. They often fell off the mule's back, so Losang's little daughter, Namgyal Drolma, helped to protect them from the rear.

To get to Dangram Village is get to the Losang's. His family includes his wife, sons, daughters, a lot of grandsons and granddaughters. As we arrived there, we saw one daughter sitting quietly outside with a child. She was not well and had just returned from seeing her husband. After the Tibetan New Year's Day, she became seriously ill and passed away. We were very sorry about that and wished that she would rest in peace. That day, after we received this information about his family, Losang took us to visit the other 16 families in Dangram. The old man was walking quite rapidly in front of us and calling out "Hello" to everyone we met, quite unlike a man of 78. Later, as we repaired our "Qulho", he often dropped in to offer a hand. Now and then, he came to see us in the village committee and did not leave until it was dark (though Dangram is about three to four kilometers from our site). Compared with other men of his age, he has a much lighter body and a rapid stride.

Losang is an old cadre in the village, but now he actually works in place of his daughter. The truth is that a woman was required when the committee was first organized yet it is not easy to find a suitable woman in the village. For this reason, Losang suggested a solution that his daughter could take the position in the committee and that he would do the job for her. Dangram is upstream from the Village of Yerpa. It is the water source for three villages on the river and there have been many local quarrels regarding inappropriate water usage. During committee meetings, when other members mentioned inappropriate water usage, he seemed to not hear well and when he spoke it appeared irrelevant to the topic. What he most often murmured was that Dangram is a small village often deceived by the larger ones and failing to get its deserved benefits. He gets into hot disputes with his colleagues, which makes us all concerned about the state of his heart.

Likewise, while representing the sixteen families of Dangram, Losang often travels back and forth on the rough mountain road from the committee to his village.

No matter whether it is winter or summer, Losang always wears a hat. We didn't pay attention to it at first, until one day when his daughter told us that as early as two years ago, when the village repaired the bridge over the Nujiang River, Losang got a small boil on his head which he scratched until it bled. Then he put cement on the wound. Later, his ulcer became bigger and bigger. When we looked at it, the boil had become as big as a coin and we became concerned. But maybe it was not a big problem.

As summer came, Losang complained of pain from this ulcer. We found it to be bleeding a little so we decided to take him to the county hospital when we went downtown for a bath and to buy vegetables. That day he had put on clean clothes as if he meant to stay for a while in the county. However, a few days later, he showed up again in the village committee. We asked him why he had come back so soon. He said that the doctor asked him to stay in the hospital for treatment, which would cost him several thousand yuan. Since his daughter had passed away earlier in the year, he had no money to pay the cooperative medical care insurance, so he came home.

How could that be? We consulted the township village office and the County Bureau of Health about his case, and were informed that it was the right time to re-apply for “NCMS” (The New Rural Cooperative Medical Care System) so we reached an agreement with the Health Department that Losang could receive treatment first, then get a reimbursement later according to regulations. My team informed his family of the news at once and asked him go to see the doctor in the county with us the next day. Tseshi, one of Losang’s daughters (who carried water for us), went home right away when she got the news. Losang came to the village committee earlier the next morning, the ulcer on his head had enlarged even more.

Losang’s little daughter, Namgyal Drolma, would go to the hospital with him. We told her to prepare some days’ clothes and food for him to save money in the county. The work team would pay for the cost for medical treatment in the hospital in advance. It was lunchtime when we arrived at the county hospital and the doctors were on break, so we arranged for the father and daughter to have lunch first, then went to Losang’s relative and waited a moment. We would go to the hospital with him in the afternoon, in case he ran away once again. After lunch, we were busy buying next week’s supply of goods and materials. Then, we called on Namgyal, Vice President of the hospital. He was a man who had affection for the common people, since he had come to Yerpa for a return medical visit and donated money to the village. Mr. Namgyal arranged for a doctor for Losang. Having seen his ulcer, the doctor said that it could deteriorate and was in danger of becoming a cancer… yet conditions in the county hospital could not permit examinations for cancers. He suggested we go to the hospital in Chamdo. It was 300 kilometers from the Pashod County to Chamdo. Yet speed was desirable so we set out right away and headed for Chamdo.

About 10:00 pm, we arrived at Chamdo and immediately went to the emergency department in the People's Hospital. The emergency department introduced us to the in-patient department of the 2nd Surgical Section. Dr. Peng examined Losang and said the same thing as the doctor in Pashod had said. We wanted Losang to be hospitalized but all the beds were occupied. Dr. Peng suggested we come back the next day at 9:00 am, when the doctors had just finished making their rounds of the wards and hadn't yet gone to operations. He intended to ask his director see Losang and made a decision. We had no choice but went to dinner and found a place to stay overnight. The next day would be a new day. From morning to night, we waited for the doctor in the People's Hospital. We had been waiting for about eight or nine hours (which, for Losang, seemed a little hard). Though tired out, he didn't vomit as most other villagers did when they got into a car; otherwise, he suffered a lot from carsickness.

The next day, we went for an appointment at the hospital. Dr. Yin saw Losang and said that he should reduce the inflammation first and then make a pathological examination. If there was no cancer he could do an operation to remove the ulcer and provide a skin graft. If it is a cancer, even the hospital in Chamdo cannot help us, the patient has to be moved to the hospital in Lhasa or in the hinterland. Upon the news, some newspaper reporters, who came for an interview, advised us to ask for financial support, otherwise, it is impossible for the Losang family to afford the resulting medical expense. We could do nothing but let him be hospitalized first. Knowing our situation, the hospital leader arranged a special bed for Losang in the Emergency Department. However, Losang didn't agree and insisted upon returning with us. We told him that we would pay his medical expenses in advance and in addition, we would return to pay them when he finished the anti-inflammation treatment and pathological examination. No matter what we said to him, he didn't respond, maybe he thought that if we left, the father and daughter would be complete strangers in Chamdo and would be helpless in the big city. This was understandable. Anyway, he had to receive treatment, so we asked the doctor in Chamdo and President Namgyal in the county hospital if Losang could go back to the county for anti-inflammation treatment, then return to the regional hospital for other treatments. They agreed.

The next day we drove back to the county hospital. A female doctor in the in-patient department received us. We told her that the doctor in Chamdo had suggested it was better not to use an anti-inflammatory medicine like cephalosporins (an anti-biotic) for more than a week, and to go on taking the drugs everyday. She replied, "We will be responsible for the remedy once the patient is here, and we have our own regimens." Then, she listened to Losang's heart and took his blood pressure carefully. Finally, she said that she was only a physician, we had to wait for a surgeon. We explained to her that we had to return to the village as soon as possible, and asked if she could arrange for Losang be hospitalized first. She answered: "Oh, you are not his family! Just leave the patient here, he is not a child." We said to ourselves that he was more childlike than most children. Having done the related procedures and paid the deposit, we told her that Losang would go back to the regional hospital for examination after the inflammation was reduced. She said, "he will be fine after the anti-inflammation treatment here, so why do you return for other examinations in the regional hospital?"

She was right.

About a month later, Losang and his daughter came home. Now in good health, he soon involved himself with village affairs again.

Issue: No.3, 2013.

22 PHENTOK'S LIFE OF CLIMBING: THE FIRST WOMAN ON THE SUMMIT OF MT. QOMOLANGMA

Text by Huang Xing & Xu Wanhu

On March 31, 2014, Phentok, the first woman mountaineer in the world to reach the summit of Mt. Qomolangma from the north side, passed away because of complications from diabetes, aged 75. From her humble upbringing as a serf to the first Chinese woman on Mt. Qomolangma, she left behind an uplifting life story.

From Serf to Mountaineer

Phentok was born in a family of serf in what is now Jomda County of Chamdo Prefecture in 1939. From the age of 6, she started her life as a young herdswoman. Her life was tough, but with two loving parents, it was also sweet. When she was 8, her father passed way. Without the pillar of the family, the young Phentok and her mother had to leave their home, and begged their way to her father's hometown of Shigatse.

Shigatse is known as the "city of mountaineers" in Tibet. The north ridge of Mt. Qomolangma, the highest peak in the world, stands here. Phentok was

Rhentok is receiving the interview. Photo by Han Yuqing

about to forge a bond with Mt. Qomolangma.

In 1950, the 11-year-old Phentok came to Shigatse. She and her mother made a living by weaving carpets, but they could hardly make ends meet. When Phentok was 12, her mother fell ill, and she was forced to assume the role of the main bread winner in the family. The next year, she left home tending cattle and sheep for the lord. Later when her mother got better, the two of them worked as porters. When her mother finally succumbed to illness exasperated by heavy labor, Phentok had to move to Lhasa and lived with a friend of her mother's. In 1958, she became a vegetable planter in Qiyi (July 1st) State Farm west of Lhasa. In that year, a life-changing event took place in her life: Xu Jing, the captain of China Mountaineering Team, came to the farm to scout for talents, and Phentok was picked.

Phentok later recalled, "Our coach was dressed in a military overcoat and military boots. Other Tibetan girls and I myself all thought he was recruiting soldiers, so we all signed up." Once she entered the team, the young

Phentok made it through the so-called "hell week", passed three rounds of eliminations with flying colors, and became a formal member of the Chinese Mountaineering Team, thus beginning her life of climbing.

Being a mountaineer was no easier than being a soldier. Once on the team, she had to undergo some intense physical training on a daily basis: besides the long-distance running, weightlifting, and pommel horse exercises, she also received rigorous climbing techniques training. Through it all, whether it was running or weight-bearing marching, she always kept pace with the male teammates.

The strict training schemes left Phentok with a high fitness level and solid climbing techniques. On Feb. 4, 1959, the 20-year-old Phentok reached the peak of Mt. Tanglabao in her first attempt at mountain climbing. From then on, this young mountaineer started a hot streak: a series of mountains over 7,000 meters high, including Mt. Muztag Ata and Mt. Gongar Jiubie, were conquered by her.

Mt. Muztag Ata is 7,546 meters high. No female mountaineer had ever reached such heights before. In the adaptive training before ascent, Phentok was hit by altitude sickness: she suffered from splitting headache, excessive heart rate, and vicious vomiting. But she just clenched her teeth and held on. On the day of ascent, Phentok and her teammates climbed up step by step against winds of force 10 and in knee-deep snow. Every one to two meters, they had to lean on their ice axes for a moment to catch their breath. Slowly but steadily Phentok and seven other female teammates climbed to the top of Mt. Muztag Ata, setting new world record on highest mountain scaled by women.

Two years later, Phentok and her teammates topped Mt. Gongar Jiubie, the 7,595-meter-high sister peak of Mt. Muztag Ata, breaking the world women's record again. But this success was a bitter one: on their descent, five teammates were killed in a snowslide. Buried in snow and suffered multiple injuries, Phentok herself only just narrowly escaped death. Whenever she talked about this tragedy later, Phentok could not hold her tears back.

The First Chinese Woman on Mt. Qomolangma

The near-death experience did not deter Phentok from going forward in her mountaineering career. In 1974, China Mixed Mountaineering Team for Climbing Mt. Qomolangma was established, and Phentok was named vice captain. They were aiming for the highest mountain on earth.

To stand on the top of Mt. Qomolangma is the ultimate dream of every mountaineer. Phentok was no exception. She was on the wrong side of 30 then, and a mother of three. Her youngest daughter was not yet weaned. After some soul-searching lying awake at nights, Phentok decided to leave the children to the care of her family, and reported to the team alone for a 6-week training program.

Tibetan female mountaineer Gosang has successfully climbed Mt. Qomolangma twice. Then 18 years old, Gosang was a teammate of Phentok on China Mixed Mountaineering Team for Climbing Mt. Qomolangma. She recalled that there was something special about elder sister Phentok. "During our weight-bearing march, she secretly put some rocks in her pocket to add the intensity."

In March of 1975, the team arrived at the foot of Mt. Qomolangma. In the early team activities, Phentok was put on the transport division responsible for the transport of supplies between Mt. Qomolangma Base Camp and the stop on 8,100 meters. "Phentok was one of the senior members of the team, but she was fully devoted to the mundane work, leading her team working in the snow. We had such admiration for her." Gosang said.

The ascent did not go as smoothly as planned. The team had to regroup. It was later cut down to a core squad for the climb. Phentok was in the squad. After 5 days of trekking, they reached the camp on 7,600 meters on May 21st. With a snowstorm raging in the background, they could only curl up in the tent with limited oxygen and food supply for three days. On the 25th, the weather improved at last. The team seized the chance and advanced to the height of 8,300 meters. On the 26th, Phentok and co finished scouting and roadwork, and reached the camp on 8,600 meters.

Once they went past the Second Step, Mt. Qomolangma was well within

After ascend the summit of Mt. Qomolangma from the north side and back to the base camp, Phentok (Left 4) and her teammates celebrated the success.

sight. However, the section between 8,680 and 8,710 meters is a 20-to-30-meter-long rock which sits almost vertically. It is called "a place where birds cannot fly through".

Phentok was passing a backpack to a teammate above her when it was somehow stuck by a rock. Pulling hard at it, she lost her balance and rolled back. Just when she was about to fall off the cliff, she had the quick wit to grab onto a protruding rock on the cliff and stuck her foot into a crack. She then managed to control her body and recovered.

"Though there was a metal ladder in place, to climb the Second Step was still extremely difficult. I was in my early twenties, and I felt that my strength was deserting me. Phentok was more than 10 years older than me, but she marched on quickly." Samdrup, who was one of Phentok's teammates then and later became captain of Tibet Mountaineering Team, recalled.

On 14:30 of the 27th, the team topped Mt. Qomolangma at last. Phentok became the first woman to successfully ascend the summit of Mt. Qomolangma from the north side. That was the peak of her life and career.

Samdrup said that while they were on the peak, Phentok lied down for over 40 minutes in the snow for a electrocardiograph test, the result of which was sent back immediately to the base camp by their portable radio transmitter. Phentok's electrocardiograph on the peak of the world is still the only one of its kind.

The Couple of Snow Mountains: A Love Tested by Wind and Snow

In 1961, during the campaign to scale Mt. Gongar Jiubie, Phentok met her Prince Charming, Deng Jiashan. Soon love blossomed between them.

Deng Jiashan then was a handsome, masculine young man of medium height. He was the vice captain of the 2nd division of mountaineering team, of which Phentok a member was. He graduated from Xi'an School of Surveying and Mapping in 1958, and later worked in National Administration of Surveying and Mapping. He was selected for mountaineering training, and was then sent to the Soviet Union for intensive training. He climbed Lenin Peak once there.

In their time together on the team, Phentok and Deng Jiashan got to know each other. They always had so many things to talk to each other and got along very well. Seeing how busy Deng Jiashan was, Phentok took on all the work such as shoveling snow, boiling water, and making meals when camping, sometimes even made the bed for him. The two shared meals and lived under the same roof. Two young hearts were joined in love.

There was one time when Phentok suffered from snow blindness and had a frostbitten toe on her way down a mountain. When she was struggling to find her way, Deng Jiashan showed up leading a horse. He gently lifted her onto the saddle and walked her back to the camp. It was a bumpy ride, but Phentok's heart was full of peace and warmth. Under Deng Jiashan's meticulous care, Phentok gradually recovered.

In 1962, Phentok and Deng Jiashan were both sent back to Tibet Mountaineering Camp. They got married the next year. Two years later, their first child was born. The newlyweds did not stay in their love nest for long. Instead, the majority of their time was dedicated to the cause of mountaineering. Because they were away from home so much, they had to put their three kids in the care of Deng Jiashan's brother and sister in Wuxi.

Though they were working for the same cause, they were often on different assignments and not together. They were deeply in love, and always rooting for each other in his/her career. Phentok and Deng Jiashan were both involved in the 1975 Mt. Qomolangma campaign, but they did not see each much. Deng Jiashan spent 5 days in the camp on 7,500 meters planning routes from the ascent team. On his way down, he bumped into Phentok and her teammates. They had not seen each other for two months. Phentok waved excitedly to her husband from a distance, but Deng Jiashan just raised his ice axe slightly pointing to the peak.

"Seeing him point his ice axe up towards the peak, I immediately got it: he wanted me to go to the top. I stared off in the direction he indicated, and saw a row of little red flags he planted as signs on the mountain road. Suddenly I could not hold my tears back. But to save energy, I only nodded to him, and we passed each other by." Phentok once recalled.

In 1980, Phentok and her husband were transferred to work in Wuxi. It was only from then on that the family was finally reunited.

Years of mountaineering exploits left Phentok and her husband with not only glories, but numerous injuries. Just like back when they climbed the mountains together, the two of them fought with pain and diseases side by side. Phentok used to say, "It was destiny that brought us together. For decades, we've been through thick and thin, always appreciating and caring for each other. Nothing can tear us apart. We have always been climbing together."

Phentok and her husband are reading the photo autobiography of phentor at home. Photo by Han Yuqing

Never-ending Climb

After her mountaineering career had ended, Phentok and Deng Jiashan went back to his hometown of Wuxi. She spent over 30 years in the region south of the Yangtze River, still working in sports, albeit in a different role. Wuxi's altitude is almost at sea level. There are no high mountains here, but she never stopped "climbing".

Deng Jiashan said that when they first relocated to Wuxi, language became a big barrier for his wife. But she made up her mind to learn the Jiangnan dialect. "Of course it was no longer mountains that we had to deal with, it was still enormously challenging especially for Phentok. But with her never-give-up spirit, she was conversing with the locals with ease in no time."

A retired employee of Wuxi Bureau of Sports said, "At first, we thought she was just a national heroine coming here to live out her life in retirement.

But we soon found that she had brought the mountaineering mentality to her work here."

Phentok retired in 1998. But she could not give up her life-long love of sports. In that year, upon the repeated requests of Cheng Biao, headmaster of Shanghai Tongzhou Model School, Phentok agreed to become the honorary president of the school. Despite the title, she was not just some celebrity lending her name to a cause, she visited the school every month.

Phentok's bravery and courage in conquering the world's highest peak inspired the teachers and students of Tongzhou. When Tongzhou Handball League was formed, Phentok was named honorary president of the league. With her effort, the number of the members of the league has grown from the original 8 to the current 100-plus.

Various honors were bestowed on her in recent years: she was one of the eight former athletes to carry the Olympic flag on the opening ceremony of the 2008 Beijing Olympics; in 2009, she was nominated as one of the most influential sports personalities of the new China...

Today, Mt. Qomolangma still stands on the roof of the world like a spear pointing to the sky. Phentok left her mark there, perhaps she is still up there watching over every mountaineer with dreams.

Issue: No.5, 2014.

23
MY COUSIN, AN EMINENT MONK

Text by Tenzin

Chapter One

The day is the fifth day of the seventh month in the Tibetan calendar. It is an auspicious day due to the Buddha having once preached on this date. After lunch, my younger cousin called from our hometown and told me that my older cousin's relic stupa had been completed and blessed. It was placed facing south on the west side of the great sutra hall of the Gonsar Monastery in which he spent all his life. It was hard to articulate my feelings since they ranged between great joy, relief, and grief. I felt as if a jewel had been lost, a ripe fruit had fallen to the ground, or a majestic snow mountain had loomed large in front of me. An enlightened follower of the Buddha walked along the celestial ladder or took a boat to reach the other side.

My older cousin was the third son of my mother's second eldest sister. He was born in 1936, but his exact birthday was unknown. Most ordinary Tibetan families do not record their children's birthdays. What they remember is usually something like "it snowed on that day", "the grass was green then", or "it was during the barley harvest season". It is said that my older cousin was born during the harvest season. His secular name was Tenpa, maybe because he was born on a Saturday (Tenpa means "Saturday" in Tibetan). When he entered the monastery, he was given the religious name Konchog Chogyal Sangpo, meaning "the wisdom of the teachings of the Buddha". His life proved that he was worthy of the name. When he was three, his parents sent him to my home to study Tibetan along with the basics of Buddhism from my father. At the age of eight, he was sent to the Gonsar Monastery to be ordained as a novice monk.

Life has no beginning and no end, like a plant growing in fertile soil under the sun and naturally bearing fruit. Life is also like a map on which there are so many roads which one can choose but with no directions provided with them. In the 1950s, the two of us entered the same monastery one after the other, where we both became students of the same living Rinpoche, studying sutras and worshipping the Buddha in the same sutra hall. However, we went our separate ways in the early 1960s. Guided by the People's Liberation Army, I left the monastery and resumed a more secular life. Then I left Tibet to go to school in the mainland. Konchog Chogyal Sangpo, however, never changed. He was always dressed in his cassock, holding prayer beads and chanting the teachings of the Buddha. He devoted his life to the study and practice of the path of enlightenment and lived an ascetic life adhering strictly to its commandments. In the end, he mastered the five sciences of ancient India and became an eminent monk highly accomplished in Buddhist studies. His exemplary conduct and nobility of character was admired by all. One day last September, I received a call from my younger cousin from the monastery. He told me that Konchog Chogyal Sangpo was seriously ill. His fellow monks, believers, friends, and family were all very concerned. The monks offered incense sticks and prayed for his recovery; believers also kowtowed and turned prayer wheels, and his family and friends all offered to send for a doctor to look for cures. The whole town was worried about the health of their great monk.

I asked my younger cousin what Konchog Chogyal Sangpo said when he found out about his condition. He said that after a Buddhist ritual, Konchog

Chogyal Sangpo told the monks around him, "When beef cattle are driven to the slaughterhouse, if they see grass and water, they seize every opportunity to take a bite or have a drink, oblivious to their imminent death. We have practiced the Buddha's teachings for our whole lives. We should know that there is no possible way to escape death. Dying is as natural as living. We are dying from the moment we are born. Life is like a doorway. It looks like an entry seen from the outside and an exit seen from the inside. I have completed my life's work, so I can face death happily."

I reflected on his words for a long time. Konchog Chogyal Sangpo remained calm in the face of death because he had found his true self. To me, he is a towering inspiration whom I can only look up to in awe, but we were of the same blood after all. I could not just let go.

I immediately called my younger cousin, telling him to ask the monk if he would like me to arrange for a doctor from Nagqu or Lhasa to visit him or if he were willing to travel to big cities like Kunming where more advanced medical facilities were available.

Konchog Chogyal Sangpo lived in a monastery where the air was thin at an altitude of over 4,200 meters above sea level. He did not eat meat and always stuck to the "no food after midday" precept, so he was probably malnourished. I rummaged through my home and found some health-food supplements like American ginseng, herba dendrobii, and spirulina, sending them out by express mail. A week later, my younger cousin called and told me that they had received the package, but the monk only took three spirulina tablets. We both knew that it was not for his illness but for the fact that they were sent from afar and that he appreciated my sentiment. He said, "Wrinkles on our face, gray hair, teeth falling out, and mind and body getting slow are inevitable natural processes. There is no immortal life just like there is no eternal oil lamp. If I die someday, it will be like an oil lamp lighting another one or a swan flying into a lotus lake. I will be filled with happiness, not sadness. If my illness does not bring trouble to others and my death does not bring sadness to others, then I will have achieved enlightenment. It would be nice if we could see each other again, though." I heard that, from then on, he stopped going to the doctor's and taking his medicine, just sitting cross-legged and peacefully meditating with his eyes closed.

I understand that a true spiritual practitioner starts practicing contemplation and meditation on death under his masters from the day he takes refuge in the Three Jewels and is initiated into monkhood. When death comes, he will not feel any pain inside. He who adheres to the Buddhist disciplines and rules is free from greed and selfish desire. Since he has not killed, he will not be troubled by hatred; since he has not stolen, he will not be caught; since he has neither lied nor said false things, he will not be estranged from friends; since he is free from lust, he will not be targeted by malicious words; and since he is free from desire, he will not be troubled by wrath. All that goes on to the next life is our mind with its karmic imprints. It is the ending of sorrow and delusion, and it is supremely peaceful. This is a special teaching of Tibetan Buddhism. We Tibetans believe that "It is only by understanding the death process that one can recognize how precious life is and live it fully". This is very different from the Chinese notion of "If you don't understand what life is, how will you understand death?" Buddhists believe that what dies is just the body, but the soul will remain. The death of a spiritual practitioner just means its soul transmigrates from one being to another. The virtuous soul will last forever.

Chapter Two

During the National Day holiday, I was required to attend a meeting in Beijing, but Konchog Chogyal Sangpo's condition gave me sleepless nights. Once the meeting was over, I bought an air ticket to Lhasa, and got up at 5 a.m. to make a run for the airport. After the 4-hour flight, I landed in Lhasa Gonggar Airport at 11. Then I got on a Toyota off-road vehicle to continue my journey.

I had not been to Tibet for three years. Autumn in Tibet is spectacularly beautiful: the clouds leisurely floating across the blue sky; the limpid river running by the vast snow mountain; the green grasses turning yellow. You cannot find such scenery anywhere else in the world. Our car sometimes went past swirls of snowy clouds, and at other times, it waded across rivers or roared its way climbing the slope. I sat by myself trying to collect my thoughts. The gentle melancholy of autumn filled my heavyhearted journey: it was like the journey of life, from restlessness to quiet, from storm to calm, from over-decoration to simplicity. What remained yours in the end were not intense emotions but eternal peace and tranquility.

The sun had set. The moon rose. Under the starry sky, I finally got home around 11 at night. The highway ended there. I did not even go home but jumped on the horse which my younger cousin had prepared for me for the last 10-plus kilometers on the mountain road to the monastery where Konchog Chogyal Sangpo lived. I used to know the road like the back of my hand, because 50 years ago I traveled on this road at least once every month. I remembered the location of every ditch and every slope. Even those big trees remained fresh in my memory, but times had changed. My hometown had changed beyond my recognition. I had to be careful with each step I took. At last, I reached the monastery. Not a sound could be heard there. The majestic calmness of the sacred place eased my fatigue from the 18-hour journey. Following Buddhist customs, I went to the Great Sutra Hall to burn incense and pay my respect before calling on the rustic weather-beaten monk dormitory.

Konchog Chogyal Sangpo's dormitory was a small house whose walls were made of rammed earth. Despite its simple and crude look, it was actually rock-solid and steady. The combined floor area of the building was less than 80 square meters. The ground floor was the storage space for firewood. There was a sutra hall on the first floor which housed statues of Guru Marpa and Milarepa. Besides the Buddha statues, the room of some 20 square meters was completely occupied by sutra books: rare books, manuscripts, and sutras of various sizes were stacked along the walls, on the table, on the niche, or lying on the windowsill. A tiny room of nine square meters next-door served as his bedroom and spiritual practice room.

I lifted the door curtain and saw Konchog Chogyal Sangpo sitting cresslegged on his square-shaped wooden bed, which was more like a wooden frame than a bed. There was something of a backrest in the back. Like most experienced monks, he never slept lying down. He was pale and emaciated, but there was a majestic air about him. His broad forehead shined. According to the sutra, this was where the all-seeing divine eye was. His dry lips moved slightly, praying for all living creatures. His long, thin, yet strong fingers counted the prayer beads which were so worn they were of different sizes. His half-closed eyes were fixed on the Thangka, *The Realm of Bliss* on the opposite wall. He looked in perfect possession of himself, fully prepared to enter the pure land of ultimate bliss. I put my palms together and said, "Brother, it's me."

His face spread into a warm smile, showing the lines on his forehead. His straight bushy eyebrows were like awns of mature highland barley. Stripes of his yellow pointed hat rested on his shoulders. Seeing his face, the anxious beatings of my heart were soothed. It was full of relief and admiration. Death is unavoidable. Different people have different views on death and different attitudes towards it. For a highly accomplished Buddhist monk, death is an opportunity to achieve enlightenment. There is no fear or sadness, just expectation in contentment.

He started to talk at last. "This is your home. It's good for you to come back." He closed his eyes, contemplated for a moment, then lifted his hands to put them together and straightened his back. I knew he was muttering the prayers for the emancipation of all living beings, including me. This was the only act of merit he could perform now and was his courteous reception of me.

It was 1:30 in the morning when I got home from the monastery. It took me a total of nineteen hours to get from Beijing to this remote corner on the Qinghai-Tibet Plateau. I had traveled over 6,000 kilometers just to see my brother.

When I woke up the next morning, my room was filled with the familiar mixture of smells of the cow dung fire, butter tea, and barley wine. It was the smell of home. I got up and opened the door to step onto the balcony.

It was a beautiful day with brilliant sunshine and a sapphire sky. Inhaling the sweet fresh air, I finally realized it was not just a dream. I was indeed in my hometown, where I was born and raised. The snow-capped peak of the holy mountain rose out of the clouds in the distance, making it difficult to distinguish between clouds and the mountain. Nearby, the greenish water of the Nu River flowed along my home. Looking east, the golden dome of the 600-year-old Gonsar Monastery loomed in the forest of cypress trees at the foot of the snow mountain by the Nu River. Across the river, over the mountains, the familiar toll of the monastery bells rang in my ears. Overwhelmed by strong nostalgic emotions, I ran up the mountain to the pile of rocks with yellow, white, and blue prayer banners planted on them. Here, the Gonsar Monastery revealed itself in front of me. The monastery sits on the slope shaped like an elephant trunk at the foot of the mountain. Its gleaming golden roof symbolizes the rank of the monastery, showing believers that this is the entrance to the realm of the Buddha. To realize enlightenment, believers should spin the prayer wheels lined side-by-side in a row by the walls and recite the six sacred words with the Buddha's teachings in mind. Behind the monastery, there is a sky burial site with white banners on the four sides. Not far from there, vultures circled over the top of the mountain, signaling the reincarnation of the soul.

No matter what changes had taken place in the outside world, for 70 years, Konchog Chogyal Sangpo remained firm in his devout, pure, and determined belief. In early 1959, when he was just 24, he had finished studying the five traditional topics of study. His grasp of Sanskrit, medicine, and mathematical science had reached a high standard. On the fifteenth day of the third month of the Tibetan calendar that year, the most important annual sutras debate meeting of the Gonsar Monastery was held. This was the most crucial moment in the life of a monk whose knowledge, eloquence, and mental strength was to be tested. Konchog Chogyal Sangpo sat by himself on the square-shaped grass mat on the sutra debate field on the left side of the Great Sutra Hall. Nearly 1,000 eminent monks from twelve monasteries were seated around him. Twelve elected examiners stood in front of him. They were an intimidating bunch: holding prayer beads, with their kasayas tucked around their waists, they often clapped their hands or stamped the ground with one foot, to raise a quick-fire series of questions. Calm, collected and quick-witted, Konchog Chogyal Sangpo always answered with confidence and grace, quoting the classics at ease and winning roars of applause and cheers. He was not only given the degree of Geshe, but also named by Riwang Rinpoche as the lead sutra chanter of the Gonsar Monastery for three years, which was an academic title second only to Tulku. On the ceremony to confer him the title, he wore a brocade coronary hat, a brand-new yellow kasaya and a pair of colorful boots which signified his status. The monks formed two lines to make a corridor. With ritual music playing and prayer banners fluttering, he walked behind the apprentice monks, transporting colorful arrows out of the dormitory, into the main hall, and mounting them on the podium. From the bottom of my heart, I admired his erudition and envied his majestic aura. I made up my mind to view him as my role model and make becoming a lead chanter my purpose in life.

Before long, a major event took place: Tibet was peacefully liberated. A platoon of People's Liberation Army soldiers with red star caps on their heads, pistols tied to their waists, and bedding rolls on their backs entered the Gonsar Monastery. They were here to establish and manage relations with the upper-class monks. My sutra teacher was the abbot of the monastery, so he was naturally the number one person with whom the PLA wanted to make friends. There were lots of vacant rooms in his large mansion, so the platoon rented all of them and settled there. I saw with my own eyes that they were highly disciplined and fine-looking individuals. Before meals, they lined up and sang songs; after meals, they cleaned the courtyard. In a word, they were not the ferocious monsters described in rumors, so I tried to approach them. Once I knew them, they inspired both affection and respect from me. I was young and impressionable, tired of the austere religious life of a monk and yearning for another kind of challenge. So I decided to leave with the PLA. When I explained my decision to Konchog Chogyal Sangpo, he was so sad and disappointed that he burst into tears. He gave me a pair of colorful boots with his trembling hands as going away presents. According to the traditional customs of my hometown, this means that no matter how far the native son has gone, he would not forget his hometown and folk. Even when he makes something of himself, he would still have his footsteps firmly planted here in the monastery. That was the most privileged and affectionate send-off anyone could receive.

Chapter Three

I came back that afternoon to check on him. Dressed in his kasaya, he was seated in the lotus position with his back straight. His cheeks were rosy, his voice clear, and his expressions unreadable. Offerings symbolizing cleanliness such as dried fruits, flowers, clear water, and white conch were placed on the square table in front of him. He gestured to the seat cushion beside him and said, "We are all just passing through this world. We cheer for life and grieve over death, often ignoring that the most important quality is actually compassion. We shall be charitable and merciful. I am going to give you a gift today, to chant the Mani sutra which I have recited countless times to give you strength." According to Buddhist rituals, this is a great honor. When you lack spiritual cultivation yourself, the merit accumulated by others can be transferred to you to plant the seeds of goodness in your heart.

Today, he was feeling better. So he performed this rare, grand, and sacred ritual, praying for all people, including me. He took out a warm-faced 33-centimeter tall Maitreya statue from the shrine and then took a vase, a bronze mirror, a vajra, and a tambourine from the leather case holding the ritual instruments, lining them up on the table covered with a yellow tablecloth. Offerings like incense, clear water, a lit oil lamp, and dried fruit were already laid there. Looking at me with compassion as well as a hint of relief and delight, he recited the prayers with dedication and respect. He looked solemn and focused, putting his hands together to pray for all sentient beings. When he held up the vase filled with water of wisdom and compassion, dipping a resplendent peacock feather in the water and scattering it in the sky, this cramped room seemed to be shrouded in exotic fragrance. I was filled with a sense of comfort, serenity, and happiness.

On my way back, I recalled our first meeting after I had left home. It was 1976; the Cultural Revolution was about to end. I graduated from the Journalism Department of Fudan University and had got a job at the newspaper *Tibet Daily*. One day, I received an unexpected call from the guard saying there was a beggar outside asking for me. I walked to the gate and saw a disheveled man carrying a dirty sack on his shoulder. His coat was so worn and darned in places that it was hard to tell its original color; his Tibetan boots were so worn that his toes were poking through. At first sight, I took him for a vagrant. It was not until much later that I recognized him: my cousin whom I had not seen in sixteen years. No wonder the guard thought he was a beggar!

We went back to my newly-assigned dorm. Twilight was falling. There was no electric light in the room, so we had to light the oil lamp. There was no butter, so I made some vegetable soup. The two of us sat face-to-face by the desk, my only piece of furniture, and poured our hearts out. The candle flickered on and on, perhaps because the oil was diluted. Two rough porcelain bowls of watery vegetable soup sat in front of us, reflecting our pale complexions like a mirror. We talked all through the night until the cock crowed. Completely exhausted, he fell asleep with his head rested on the desk.

What he had gone through all those years flashed through my mind. In the catastrophic decade, this virtuous monk kept a firm guard on his faith, maintained a pure heart, and unflinchingly lived up to his promise as a devoted Buddhist.

Soon after I left the monastery, the soldiers left too. The monastery did not suffer any damage, but religious activities dropped significantly. The people's freedom of religious belief was protected, but half the monks resumed secular life. Konchog Chogyal Sangpo and dozens of devout apprentice monks stuck with their beloved monastery through thick and thin. In late 1966, the whirlwind of the Cultural Revolution hit the tiny village with full force. In

The colorful prayer flags. Photo by Wang Shouming

the blink of an eye, black was white and up was down; the old world simply fell apart. A team of Tibetan young men wearing old military uniforms with yellow satchels stormed into the Gonsar Monastery waving their bronze-buckled belts, and a group of local farmers came in with them. Some of them had pickaxes; some carried shovels, and others had empty sacks. They used to be perfectly good-mannered Buddhists, but now they were belligerent mobsters. They started from the great sutra hall by taking the roof off, tearing down the walls, and breaking the windows. They tied a rope around the neck of a statue, pulled it down, and chopped at it with their axes, creating loud clanks of metal on metal. The shredded pages of books fluttered in the sky. Statues and sutra splints were thrown in the fire, sparks and ashes swirling in the wind.

This army of destruction camped in the sutra debate field in the monastery. When they left two months later, what remained of the Gonsar Monastery were just some ruined walls. Konchog Chogyal Sangpo did not shed any tears. As fire tries gold, so does adversity try virtue. One by one, he found the fractured sutra books, dilapidated statues, and scattered instruments, and he carefully wiped the dirt off them. He cut his kasaya into pieces and stuffed them into an ox-hide bag. Each day, he anxiously waited for the night to fall. For him, nighttime was more precious than daytime, because only in the darkness could he move these treasures passed down by his ancestors to some faraway caves. Every night, he walked on the steep mountain track for almost 30 kilometers, carrying the heavy load of religious instruments and sutra books on his back, and he put them in a cave at the foot of the holy mountain. Sometimes, he made two journeys in one night. Only the stars saw him trudge along in the mud, and only the moon lit the rugged mountain road beneath his feet.

Unfortunately, the peaceful days were only brief. One day, three armed Red Guards came to what was left of the monastery and found Konchog Chogyal Sangpo living in a tent pitched against a broken wall. They held him at gunpoint and took him to people's commune as if he were a spy. He used to be someone people looked up to, but then he was a lowly prisoner.

It was particularly hard for him when there was pouring rain and he could only listen to the howling wind in his cell, feeling as if his heart was pierced by arrows and cut through by knives. His heart wrenched when thinking of those treasures buried in the dirt and exposed to the sun and rain, but his faith never faltered. Like the sun always rises in the east and sets in the west, rivers always flow toward the sea, Buddha, Dharma, and Sangha are eternal. He could only pray, pray, and pray some more, wishing that Buddha, Dharma, and Sangha would always be the food for the hungry, water for the thirsty, warmth for the cold, a helping hand for the helpless, and a companion for the lonely, as the Buddha's light illuminates everywhere and gives relief and help to all mortal beings.

Konchog Chogyal Sangpo might have seemed resigned or even submissive on the surface, but deep down, he was hard as nails. Those in charge were unable to break him, so they sentenced him to "reform through labor", which meant herding horses for the commune. He accepted it without any grudge or complaint. It was true that he had lost his freedom, but he considered himself lucky because he was given a chance to work while admiring the beauty of nature. He saw it as a blessing. He took over the job calmly and set off every day before daybreak with a Buddha statue and the incomplete sutra book *Eighty Thousand Odes* found in the ruins of the monastery. Once they were on the pasture with abundant water and lush grass, the horses leisurely grazed in fields, and he sat down cross-legged on the grass. He stacked some rocks to make a pedestal and placed the statue on it, and he then opened his sutra book and read it aloud. Under the blue sky, his Buddhist faith became even stronger. When he went back in the evening, he hid the sutras and statues in the pack basket filled with grass. Day after day, year after year, the horses were kept plump and sturdy, and the *Eighty Thousand Odes* were etched in his memory. At last, the old policies were dismantled; he was praised for his effort, and his "reform" came to an end.

Maybe his luck turned or his prayers were answered, but Konchog Chogyal Sangpo regained his freedom, and people no longer discriminate against him. He kept his master's teachings in mind: "We are fortunate to be given this able body. We should search the true meaning of life to attain enlightenment for the benefit of all sentient beings." He then embarked on a seven-year-long journey as a wandering ascetic.

Chapter Four

His first stop was the Drowolong Monastery, the birth place of Marpa Lotsawa, the founder of the Kagyu Sect, one of the four major schools of Tibetan Buddhism. Konchog Chogyal Sangpo had to cross the vast Changtang grassland, the snowy mountains of Mount Nyanchen Thanglha, and along the wild Yarlung Zangbo Canyon.

Born into an affluent family in 1012, Marpa was exceptionally intelligent from early childhood. A wild and untamed character, he studied hard but liked to argue with others. His parents sent him to India, where he studied under the renowned guru Shakya Yeshe. Marpa made three trips to India and stayed there for 22 years. He practiced Esoteric Buddhism in his retreat, and eventually became well versed in the depths of Buddhist theory and magic until his name was revered across all Tibet. One day, in the Drowolong Monastery, where he acted as the abbot, he performed a remarkable act of transferring a soul into another body. On the gangway next to his cell, a female pigeon had just died, with many squabs chirping around the body of their mother. Master Marpa just watched the dead bird calmly and patiently when, suddenly, the pigeon jumped up, flapping her wings. The squabs were overjoyed. The onlookers turned their heads and saw Marpa himself had stopped breathing. People were in awe of his power of transferring souls and revered him as their spiritual leader.

For his trip to such a holy site, Konchog Chogyal Sangpo chose prostration, the most sublime but also most difficult way. The Gosar Monastery and the Drowolong Monastery are over 700 kilometers apart, and he embarked on the journey with one of his pupils. They put on protective leather aprons and mitts on their hands and hit the road with a handcart filled with the simplest of kitchenware. To perform a full prostration, they started out with their hands together as in prayer, raised them slightly over their heads and touched them to the top of their heads, foreheads, and then chests. Next, they dropped to their knees and flung their bodies forward. Then they stood up, took three small steps, and repeated the sequence. When he was faced with rivers without bridges, he would assess their width and make up for the distance once he waded across them. On downward slopes, as long as his body could stand it, he would slide down facedown. At nightfall, they would camp on the spot whether it was close to a village or not, with the sky as their roof and the ground as their bed. They would stop and cook meals and rest by the stream or river. During this 700-kilometer trek, Konchog Chogyal Sangpo endured the harsh winter, welcomed the spring of rebirth and renewal, enjoyed the warm and sweet summer, and experienced the autumn when everything withers. He witnessed the changes of seasons, weathered the wind, rain, snow, and frost, walked and fell prostrate all the way, and felt the pulse of the land with his heart. True belief ran in his veins and rested in his soul, with the Buddha's wisdom filling his mind. Wild animals, pouring rain, biting wind, physical fatigue, shortage of clothing and food, none of them felt like pain or torture to him, but they were rather an accumulation of virtue, experience and happiness. After over two years on the road, he reached his destination on a sunny morning. Colorful prayer banners were placed outside the Drowolong Monastery, and the wind carried beneficent vibrations across the countryside, expressing the good in human nature. The banners fluttered in the wind by the rivers, on the mountains, and around the monasteries, conveying the people's prayers to nature.

The mountains of the snow-covered plateau are scattered with numerous temples and monasteries. They are a miracle onto themselves. There are countless imposing holy mountains and sacred lakes shrouded in mystery. The most moving stories in Tibet are all about preaching Buddhism. The most magnificent buildings are all monasteries. The highest authorities are the gods, and the most devout acts are pilgrimages. Konchog Chogyal Sangpo abandoned his cart, put his sack on his back and set off. Walking with a cane, he visited one monastery after another. At the feet of the important sacred mountains, he would fall prostrate, burn incense, pray, and walk around them. He poured his heart out to the holy mountains, waiting for guidance from the gods. Every grain of dust here reflects marvelous lights. On many ridges, there are large mounds of Mani stones inscribed with six-syllable mantras. Some of these mounds are as big as sheep, and all pilgrims circumventing the mountains would marvel at the sight of them, their hearts filled with compassion and cleared of false thoughts. Some yak skulls inscribed with sutra texts are placed on the top of the Mani stone mounds. Years of exposure to the sun, wind and rain leave the skulls bleached so white, giving them an appearance of ivory. These animals were given some personality or even spirituality thanks to their association with sutra texts. I believe they would be reincarnated as humans in the next life. The Mani stones, touched by countless hands, have witnessed so many human stories over the centuries. They are like guardians protecting the eternal holy mountains.

There are many mysterious sites used for spiritual practice in the thick forests deep in the mountains of Tibet. These dark caves or naturally-formed deserted grottoes all have beautiful surroundings, with either towering ancient trees, clear spring water, or rare stones and exotic animals. After a year of trudging in the mountains, Konchog Chogyal Sangpo reached the cave once occupied by the great master, Milarepa. A snowy mountain on which eagles fear to perch stands proudly. Luxuriant trees thrive on the mountainside. In the forest, there is a cave with one side is made from rock. This is where Milarepa spent his final 22 years meditating. Konchog Chogyal Sangpo saw this master as his parent of rebirth and believed that it was this master's teachings that brought him this far. This was the sacred site he dreamed of many times. Shedding tears of joy, he sat down cross-legged in front of the cave and took out his religious instruments. Shaking the jingles of the tambourine with his right hand and rattling the vajra with his left, he sang Milarepa's prayer song so loudly that his high resonating chanting reverberated across the valley.

This is a must-see location for all traveling monks. In the year 982, the great Tibetan tantric master Milarepa achieved enlightenment right at this site. Milarepa was orphaned at a young age and was horribly mistreated by his relatives. When he grew up, he left home to study sorcery and took his vengeance on his enemies. Under the tutelage of Marpa, he made amazing progress as a Buddhist. Marpa saw his extraordinary wit and perseverance, so he not only taught the young man everything he knew, but he also personally ordained him. In the end, Milarepa came to meditate at this cave. Once, he lit an altar lamp filled with butter and placed it on his head. He meditated day and night, sitting completely still until the butter in the lamp was exhausted. After eleven months, he was able to change his body at will and levitate through space. His heart was as pure as lotus petals. From then on, he renounced worldly desires and decided to devote his life to the spreading of the Buddha's teaching. In this holy yet mysterious cave, Konchog Chogyal Sangpo followed Milarepa's footsteps and started his two years of meditation. Apart from some fried powder of highland barley, he did not have any extra food. On the stone slab serving as his bed in the cave, he laid down a sheepskin and sat cross-legged on it. He placed his hands under his abdomen, kept his back straight, and focused his eyes on a statue of Gautama Buddha placed in front of him. Envisioning bodhisattvas and their compassion, he sat quietly and slowly ascended into a state of supreme harmony. Negative emotions like anger and greed had no place in his mind. Over two years, he subsisted on spring water and fried barley powder. Sometimes he would also go into the nearby woods and grab some wild herbs to eat.

One day not long before his two-year meditation period was about to be complete, when he was walking in the woods, he ran into a few shepherd boys. Thin as a rake, with ragged clothes and disheveled long hair, he scared the kids senseless. They ran back to the villages screaming that there was a wild man on the mountain. The news of village boys running into a wild creature traveled fast with all sorts of fabricated details added, until one day, the village sent some men to check it out on the mountain. When they learned of Konchog Chogyal Sangpo's story, they were all filled with awe and delight. Deeply moved, the villagers sang praise of this flag-bearer of Buddhism, who in the darkest of hours, still clung to his faith. The power of belief is like fertile land on which a seed will take root and flourish. The villagers, young and old, came to the cave to see the monk and listen to his preaching. After his two years of meditation, he gained a definite understanding of the Buddhist way. In front of the cave, he conducted a prayer meeting for the villagers. He took apart his rosary consisting of 108 prayer beads and gave each bead to his audience as a souvenir. Then he set out with his backpack and walking stick for his next journey.

I only knew snippets of his seven years of traveling life. According to his students, they traveled thousands of miles, visited more than 100 holy mountains and lakes, and went to 300 monasteries.

What Konchog Chogyal Sangpo told me when he said goodbye to me in my dorm later became my motto. He told me, "You are a public servant employed by the government. Be a good man. I know how to be a good Buddhist: do not kill, you will live a long and healthy life; do not steal, you will be well-fed and well-clothed; do not engage in improper sexual conduct, you will find peace in your home; do not make false statements, you will not be wrongly accused; do not envy others, you will win respect; refrain from anger, you will be happy; do not be driven by greed or lust, you will be safe from harm; in a word, do good deeds, give cheerfully and accept gratefully. I do not know what qualities a good public servant should have, but if you can do as I told you, you will certainly be someone useful to our country."

The unprecedented ten-year catastrophe came to an end at last. Those who could not raise their heads like seedlings beaten down by the frost could now stand up and hold their heads high like bamboo shoots after a spring rain. The Buddhist belief has had roots deep in the soil of the snow-covered plateau for a thousand years. Now, it is like a river running wild with unstoppable force after a harsh winter. The teachings of the masters are spread to all corners of the land. The majestic buildings of the monastery are renovated. The monks who endured hardships and kept their faith firm as ever have started preaching the teachings of the Buddha again. What is reasonable is real; that which is real is reasonable. A civilization that had been vibrant for over a thousand years would not be crushed by some intimidating slogans.

Konchog Chogyal Sangpo turned to the Gonsar Monastery and immediately began to spearhead the effort to rebuild it from the ruins. He and his fellow monks went to the villages seeking donations by performing religious services. With the money they saved up, they built the simple and quiet monk cells. Some monks who had left but had not yet resumed civilian life came back. Soon, a great sutra hall which could sit 1,000 people was built. Its interior was decorated with dazzling beautiful murals, and the imposing statues of the Four Heavenly Kings were set by its gate. When dawn breaks, as the melodious blowing of conch shells ring to the top of the sutra hall, monks dressed in crimson robes rush out of their cells looking for their own mats in the hall.

Another ten years went by. Amazingly, the sky seemed to be even more crystal clear, the sun even brighter. Sometimes, true feelings could not be put into words, but the heartfelt smiles on people's faces did not lie. The Gonsar Monastery was completely rebuilt. The snowy peaks behind it were majestic and sparkling white, while the dark mountains in the surrounding area were as imposing as iron walls. Believers came from all corners of Tibet, some on horseback, some with their cows, to attend the annual prayer meeting held in the square of the monastery. This boisterous crowd kept the place busy and full of life. The Riwang Living Buddha and Konchog Chogyal Sangpo conducted the Abhisheka ritual for some believers. Mandalas made from colored sand, a treasured vase embedded with gems, and colorful arrows rolled in colorful silk strips were blessed by eminent monks and shown to the public for the first time. Grand religious ceremonies, prayer meetings, and alms-giving assemblies were held as an appreciation of the believers' unwavering faith. The beautiful mandala was ceremonially destroyed and released back into the river. People held the colorful arrows up and touched them on their foreheads, drinking the clean water from the treasured vase. This complex yet orderly ceremony cleansed people's bodies and minds, empowering them. It aimed to bring kind-hearted longevity, contented happiness, realizing the wishes of the wise. Soon after, Konchog Chogyal Sangpo switched to a vegetarian diet where he would not eat after noon, and he retreated into his tiny room of nine square meters, where he stayed for three years, three months, and two days.

Chapter Five

On the afternoon of the third day after my arrival, I came to say goodbye to Konchog Chogyal Sangpo. I was leaving the next day and knew this might very well be our last meeting. Too ill to talk, he was sitting uptight with his eyes half-closed. I looked around this run-down room: besides several Buddha statues, there were books, old patched-up monk robes, a wooden bowl which appeared shiny after over 50 years of wear, and a threadbare sheepskin cushion on the bed. All of his possessions put together would not be worth 1,000 yuan. As if seeing through my mind, his student and personal assistant Yonten brought out a stack of thick account books whose pages were filled with closely-written Tibetan letters about the donations made by the believers. I leafed through them. From as much as 50,000 to as little as one or two yuan, every item with the names and wishes of the donors, and the amount of their donation was carefully documented.

Yonten told me that over the last 30 years Konchog Chogyal Sangpo had received about 6 to 7 millions in donation, but had never spent a cent on himself. Usually he stuck to a principle of not touching the money, which was all handled by his students. He often told them, "Alms given by the believers are not for us monks, but to the Buddha; the donation for the funeral services are not us monks, but to the Buddha too; the donation to the monastery are not for us either, all the money should be used to build and renovate the monastery." Konchog Chogyal Sangpo also took out a significant amount to help the disabled and families with financial difficulties. He often said that "the worship of Buddha is not for the successes in politics and business, but for the cultivation of respect and faith; merit gained by donating to the poor, the weak, the disabled, and the childless far exceeds that of offerings to Buddha, Dharma, and Sangha. Remember, those people might have been your parents in your previous lives." He supported over 30 elderly people living alone by providing them with food and clothing. The Buddha statue he built in the center of the great sutra hall is two storeys high, sitting on a big eightfold lotus throne lifted by 3 lions, inlaid with sparkling Mani beads, and covered with mat of lotus, sun, and moon patterns. The Buddha sits cross-legged holding the wheel of the dharma in his right hand symbolizing the continuous turning of the wheel and the dharma bells in his left hand standing for mercy, testimonies, and teachings. The statue looks both dignified and warm. Tibetans Buddhists believe that Vairocana Buddha is the highest Buddha of Tibetan esotericism. His light of wisdom shines upon all in the world, day and night, everywhere, to draw out the innate Buddhahood in both sentient and non-sentient beings. "The Buddha's light illuminates all the dharma-realm to give play to the roots of goodness in all sentient beings so they would do more good deeds in the world." Perhaps this was also the original intention of Konchog Chogyal Sangpo when he had the statue built. The huge Thangka "Buddhas of the three times" (over 3 meters tall) painted by him is hung between two thick pillars in the great sutra hall. Its hardwood roller is as thick as an arm, its yellow silk cover dazzlingly bright, and two red silk ribbons flow elegantly over it. Under the cover there are images painted with pigment of natural minerals: the Medicine Buddha of the eastern pure land, Amitabha Buddha of the western pure land, and Shakyamuni Buddha of the world. The vivid and lively images evoke admiration from everyone.

Why did he paint "Buddhas of the three times"? My guess is that it is connected to the fact that Medicine Buddha once made a vow to heal beings born with deformities, illness or other physical sufferings, to help relieve the destitute and the sick, and to help the oppressed be free from suffering. Those believers with illness and distresses would have monks come over to chant *Sutra of the Vows of the Medicine Buddha*, light the seven-layered rotating lamp, and hang the five-colored longevity banner in the hopes that their illness will be cured. Sakyamuni once vowed to relieve all sentient beings of sufferings and save all of them with a merciful and fearless heart. Amitabha stands for wisdom. He teaches people to tap into their unlimited potential to

eliminate the hindrances of karma caused in previous lives and the hindrances of partial knowledge to obtain joy and wisdom. Whether one's prayers were answered, one might have different opinions and interpretations. However, here, when you saw a solitary elderly monk pray for all beings with a heart as lofty as gold, as pure as white conchs, and as transparent as clear water, you could not help but be touched.

The gold lamp made of one kilogram of gold commissioned by Konchog Chogyal Sangpo is placed on the offering table. A monk is responsible for adding oil to the lamp, making it an ever-burning lamp. The flickering spark on the tip of the wick is like the merciful heart of an aging monk. The sutras say that there are 1, 008 Buddhas in the world, and they would all descend to the world. It was only then that the human beings could gain the final enlightenment. By then the world would become a pure land of peace and happiness, where people have gotten rid of the hindrances of desire, anger, and ignorance. But that would be an infinitely long process. There are Buddhas of three times. The past was the age of Dipamkara. 10,000 years ago, that was a happy time of no war atrocities or no wealth gap. Now is the time of Sakyamuni. It will last several thousand years. We will have to endure disasters like wars, plagues, floods, and earthquakes, and only by being merciful and doing good deeds could we alleviate the suffering. What we are looking forward at is the age of Maitreya, a time of fertility, abundance, and fraternity, i.e. an age of perfect bliss. The Tibetans are a kind-hearted and optimistic people. Devoutly religious and grateful for the now, they look to the future full of hope. My cousin Konchog Chogyal Sangpo was one of them.

Chapter Six

I left home on the morning of the forth day by flying from Lhasa to Chengdu. My phone started ringing as soon as I got off the plane. My younger cousin sobbed, "Our brother, the monk, passed away this morning at six." This did not come as a surprise to me. I was neither shocked nor particularly sad. When the world first came into being, 1,002 golden lotuses arose from the ocean. This auspicious sign was an indication of the 1,002 Buddhas who would brighten the world. Sakyamuni was the fourth of them. 108 Buddhist scholars also arrived from south of the Himalayas and took the Buddhist teachings to the snow-covered plateau. Today, Buddhists all over the world like to string 108 beads together to finger them or either wears them around their wrists or necks. The prayer beads are something they treasure and pass on. True believers accept death as part of life, so they perform good deeds to accumulate merits in life, believe the karmic retribution of sin, and see death as a passage from the burden of earthly life to the blissful pure land. It is a natural phenomenon, not unlike the blooming and fading of flowers or sunrise and sunset. That is how a Buddhist can be free from suffering and obtain great bliss. Therefore, I was not too grief-stricken for Konchog Chogyal Sangpo's passing. I just prayed for his soul.

Later, my younger cousin kept me updated with the funeral arrangements. Konchog Chogyal Sangpo's body was set on the wood bed in his dorm and given the full honor according to Tibetan Buddhist ritual procedures: a ceremonial monk hat, a yellow robe, and a silk veil. Incense sticks and candles were lighted in the room, and fruits were offered. Tulkus and eminent monks came to chant the sutra of offering incense day and night. The believers streamed in and out to pay their respects. They kowtowed and offered incense in tears. They revered him who lay in honor for 22 days, until the monastery picked an auspicious good day for the grand cremation ceremony. On the ground near the monastery, a platform was set up using rocks and bricks. Its surface was covered with a layer of sand arranged in the shape of the Tibetan word "a", and clear outlines of auspicious patterns were drawn with white chalk. A square stage for cremation was built with boards with sutras written on them. The body was placed on a wood stand. As over 100 senior monks started chanting soothing and solemn prayers accompanied by the beatings of drums and gongs, the fire was lighted. To the rich and dignified religious music, the smoke slowly spiraled up like sea waves or fogs in the wilderness into the distant sky.

Riwang Rinpoche picked up many crystal-like bead-shaped relics in the resulting ashes. To commemorate him, and to show their appreciation and admiration, the monastery had Konchog Chogyal Sangpo's relic stupa built. The shape of the stupa is based on Buddhist philosophy. The square base stands for the earth; the steps in the middle part represent four steps of attaining enlightenment; the hemispherical dome symbolizes water; the thirteen rings on the spire represent fire; the crescent moon on top represents air; and the sun stands for space and spirit. Earth, water, fire, air, and space are like a person's journey consisting of birth, life, death, and spirit (i.e. the eternal circle of life).

Since the time when Buddhism was introduced to Tibet, ancient Tibetans, with their wisdom, diligence, and courage, had managed to extract gold from gold-bearing rocks and fished precious materials from the lakes. With their wonderful workmanship, they also built countless sacred stupas, which displayed the power of Buddhist art and the eternity of life.

Stupas, sutras, and statues symbolize the body, mouth and mind (deeds, discourses, and ideas) of the Buddha. Each stupa has its own story: a new life comes into the world unpolished and untainted; he lives a hard life with the utmost discipline; and he attains enlightenment and becomes a lofty, saintly man with a pure heart. The stupa of my brother is small, simple, and unadorned, containing only his ashes and usual religious instruments; just like when he was alive, his tenacious and devout soul was wrapped in ragged clothes.

Issue: No.4, No.5, No.6, 2015.
No.1, No.2, No.3, 2016.

24

OUR STORIES OF TIBET

— An Interview with Three Foreign Students at Tibet University

Text & Photo by Dawa Yangjen & Lozang Samdro

It is a sunny, early-spring morning, and three foreign students from different countries have just arrived at the new Tibet University campus.

Linda: I Am Pema Metok from Northern Tibet

From the very end of the foreign student dormitory building comes one student in front of the others, and that is Linda from Indonesia.

On the Classroom's blackboard, Tibetan phrases can be seen everywhere. It seems as if a Tibetan class has just finished. Linda's class has eight students in total, and each of them has his or her own Tibetan name. She introduces herself in an intriguingly distinct foreign-sounding Tibetan. "I am Pema Metok, a girl from northern Tibet. My name was given to be by a nun from Xungse Monastery in Lhasa when I went there for a visit. I like my name very much."

When she arrived in 2011, she fell in love with the area. Soon after her first trip, Linda started to look up different bits of information through various channels, and in the end, she decided to apply to study abroad. After waiting a long time and passing several examinations, she eventually realized her

Linda is fond of mountain climbing.

dream of becoming a foreign student at Tibet University.

"At the very beginning, my mother was completely against my decision, so I tried my hardest to convince her and told her how I d reamed to visit Tibet." Linda did not stop chasing after her dream, though, but, "Mom thinks girls have to keep marriage and kids in mind for when they grow up!" Upon saying this, Linda bursts into laughter.

From Indonesia to Tibet is a big step from nearly sea level to the highlands, and it was certainly a major adjustment for Linda, with the altitude taking her a long time to get used to. When recalling her trouble adapting after first arriving at Tibet, Linda seems to brush it off. "That was all really nothing. I have to overcome some difficulties to be strong in the future!"

Linda likes her campus environment, and in particular, she is fond of studying Tibetan in Lhasa. Classes for foreign students are usually small. The daily curriculum for teaching mainly focuses on Tibetan culture, folkloric stories, and oral communication. Linda has yet to be absent. "Although we are from different countries, we help each other and cooperate to make

Linda showes her cooking skill to the author.

Linda likes to play the six-stringed instrument.

ourselves better." Linda comments that foreign students live harmoniously, as if the four figures described in Tibetan legends from days long past (the elephant, monkey, white rabbit, and bird) have reappeared in modern daily campus life. These students work and progress together, maintaining a peaceful environment, but upon hearing our compliments on her strenuous learning and her ability to use Tibetan and understand Tibetan culture, yet another laugh can be heard echoing throughout the classroom.

Linda has a rich array of extracurricular activities. She likes riding her bike, climbing mountains, taking bus rides, chatting in sweat-tea house, and walking around the Barkor Market. "I really like the mountains around Lhasa City and have climbed many of them," Linda says while staring out the window toward the mountains. "I enjoy looking over the city. It's truly an amazing feeling"

In the Tibet University, foreign students have an individual kitchen. Apart from cooking traditional Indonesian snacks, Linda has learned to cook Tibetan food and also makes ice cream. Her classmates like her cooked foods and appreciate her skills. Just like other girls, Linda is fond of colorful Tibetan robes, too, having bought four robes in different styles. She loves Tibetan culture, not only in terms of learning Tibetan, but also becoming involved in different cultural practices and events, such as learning to play a traditional six-stringed instrument and sing Tibetan songs. It is not unordinary to find her singing, "Gya Wa Lha Nyi-Ji Wa Lha!"

Linda likes studying and living in Tibet, and she prefers to share these very feelings with her family. During holiday breaks, she always prepares a variety of Tibetan specialties for her loved ones at home. "I brought home some caterpillar fungus for my mother once. Several days later, my mother had a 'fire' imbalance (a term within traditional medicine). Having been in Tibet for so long, I forgot Indonesian weather was actually hot!" Linda laughed, with a hint of a devious air.

When talking about living in Tibet, Linda describes her experience as "balanced". "In Tibet, it's not hard to have a balanced life. Here, people live in harmony, and life is really quite wonderful. Tibet is constantly changing, and the people' s lives are becoming better and better. I believe that better lives allow people to pay more attention to harmonious development and focus more on preserving and carrying on the traditional Tibetan Culture."

Kelly: My Life is Closely Connected with Tibet

Kelly always gives people the feeling that she is an astute and orderly American girl. On her Tibetan-style tea table, she has a cup of hot tea prepared. Her room is decorated with Tibetan-styled items, and Tibetan cultural elements are scattered everywhere. It really would not be much of a guess to say that she is interested in the Tibetan culture.

Despite her short time learning Tibetan, Kelly is eager to introduce herself

Kelly in Tibet.

in the new language. Just as the other classmates, Kelly has her own Tibetan name: Pasang, which means that her birthday falls on a Friday.

Kelly comes from California. Ten years ago, she traveled to Tibet for the first time. During this trip, she met a man named Mike from Australia. They fell in love and eventually became married. The two now have two children.

Mike is a foreign teacher at the Tibet University, and in 2016, the couple brought their children to the region. They learn the local language at the university, with Mike in particular studying the Lhasa dialect and Tibetan lexicology and Kelly studying as a beginner. Free time is usually spent with their children.

Australia to Lhasa is also nothing to laugh at in altitude difference, so when coming to Lhasa, the family made the decision to spend a couple of days in the city of Xining within Qinghai Province to adjust to the air there.

Kelly believes that Tibetan is the most difficult language to learn in the world. Equipped with what she learns in the classroom, she makes a great deal of effort trying to figure out the differences between dialects, and her

The family enjoy their leisure in the sweet tea house.

Kelly's daughters and their Tibetan friends.

passion is palpable when explaining her fascination of the varied distinction between "yes" and "no" within the Lhoka and Chamdo areas alone.

In her daily life, Kelly prefers to take her children to watch how to make butte red tea, weave, craft some traditional products, and perform other such skills. She believes that up-close-and-personal observation of how people live will allow her to gain a much deeper understanding of the local culture. Everything about daily life is interesting to her. From weddings and funerals to salt, soybean, and vinegar production, the people of Tibet use their hands to decorate their daily lives.

Perhaps it is the stark contrast between her native and this new culture that allows Kelly to see these differences so well, but she and her family truly long for the nomadic life. Whenever grassland, tents, and yaks are mentioned, Kelly's heart jumps eagerly in yearning. She says that the US and Australia do not really provide much of an opportunity to see herders in action, and so, the exotic aspect of Tibetan herders' lives is extremely interesting in her view. Black grassland tents are made of yak wool, and butte red oil comes first from yaks and is produced into variously sized blocks. "Tibetan people use natural resources in an extremely efficient way but are never too extreme in using them. It all works out perfectly! They are amazing at being able to use what is available around them," Kelly says admiringly.

"Everyone in my family loves Tibetan fabrics. They are amazingly unique in how they are patterned and designed. That's all not to mention the different kinds of Tibetan robes, the cute little colorful pigtails on girls' heads in Shigatse, and the ornaments on Khampa girls. Everything is just so special!"

One teaches while the other studies. So, who takes care of the kids? Unlike other places in China, there is no special school for foreign children. Kelly shows me two textbooks brought in from overseas. "We do homeschooling, but we make it feel like a real school". She sees my puzzled expression and explains that in many Western countries, several families have taken a liking to teaching their children at home apart from public and private education, but learning is not all about books. The couple wants to show their kids what life is like in the real world first hand so that they can learn from such experiences.

Having spent a significant amount of time in Tibet up till now, their two daughters have already learned some Tibetan. The oldest, an eight-year-old, is able to eat up ten steamed buns with mutton, and the six-year-old loves traditional sweet tea and noodles. Like other children of their age, they love Tibetan arts and the six-stringed lute-like instrument. Kelly believes Tibet is a wonderful place for her children to grow up and hopes they can continue to live there in the future.

When talking about how things are different between Tibet and Western countries, what Kelly says is quite profound. "Tibetans focus more on the family. This is quite different from the West. In Tibet, people like to communicate with each other and exchange views and ideas. Their social relations show genuine harmony." She later says, Tibetans are always kind and modest, rarely masking how they truly feel. No matter if they are poor or rich, people love to share what they have among themselves. They attach less importance to material things, so I guess you could say they are happy with what they have."

Kelly also took some time to talk about a few of the great changes that have taken place quite recently in Lhasa. When she was visiting ten years ago, there were no five-star hotels anywhere in the city, and her current campus was desolate. That is obviously not the case today. Modern conveniences are now flourishing, and public transportation is booming. The living environment and quality of life in general has taken a sharp turn for the better, in particular regarding the harmonious change in styles of living and the people's common ideology.

In Kelly's eyes, Lhasa is unique when compared with cities throughout the rest of the world. She wishes people living here will continue to have better lives and look after the environment, caring for the deep blue sky with their deeply precious hearts.

Jessica in Lhasa.

Jessica: From the Country with a Thousand Islands to the Roof of the World

Jessica comes to Lhasa from Finland, having studied in Tibet two years already. Before this, she stayed for some time in Chengdu, Sichuan Province, and during that period, she got to know a few Tibetan friends. This gave her a spark of interest to learn Tibetan and understand Tibetan culture, and it was not long before she chose Tibet University in Lhasa as her educational destination.

Jessica at the opening ceremony of the sports games in the Tibet University.

Jessica is immensely proud to have the opportunity to study Tibetan in the Tibet University. Every time she goes back to her home country, she always likes to initiate long discussions with her older sister, who is currently majoring in linguistics.

Jessica is currently learning as a beginner. Grammar is not much of a major difficulty for her, and the small classes and university-arranged extra partner-based oral practice activities are the perfect milieu for speaking and communicating with teachers and students. This beautiful situation allows for students to support each other in their learning and progress quicker and further than in many other settings.

On the table, there is a book with the title *The Legendary Epic of King Gesar*. Jessica says this book was given to her by a Tibetan friend, who specifically chose it to improve her understanding of Tibetan culture to a much deeper level. To help her grasp many of the concepts with regard to her current linguistic ability, the friend took the time to find an appropriate English version.

Jessica likes to spend her free time chatting With friends in sweat tea house, which can be found Pretty much everywhere throughout Lhasa proper. This, to her, is the best place to practice oral Tibetan. "In Lhasa, you have plenty of time to go to the sweat tea house to practice. Everyone is very patient and willing to help you."

Jessica's Tibetan name is Yeshe Tsomo. She says "Yeshe" is phonologically similar to her real name "Jessi", and "Tso" means "lake," reminiscent of her native country of a thousand lakes. Like her other two classmates, coming from a place of a thousand lakes to the roof of the world was definitely a major adjustment for her, and she found major difficulty in accomplishing this. She loves outdoor activities, but in Lhasa, she was hesitant about going out for a run or even doing a bit of exercise under the sun, which is remarkably strong and vicious so far above sea level.

"Finland has prolonged winters from November to April, and so, Finnish people dream of warm weather. They typically like to go bask in the sun in southern Europe, particularly Spain, during the winter holidays, but for me, in Lhasa, I can bask wherever and whenever I like." lt seems that Jessica's troubles from before have long since receded, and she has rather become quite fond of the great amount of sunlight now available to her.

She points to a picture hanging on the wall, in which a wooden hut stands beside a lake. "In Finland, many people love living near lakes to take in the beauty of nature, but in Lhasa, urban or rural life is both appealing to me." Although her grandfather is now getting on in years, Jessica still dreams of bringing him to Tibet so that he can enjoy its charming natural wonders.

After two years of study and living in Lhasa, Jessica loves her new home. "I feel that Tibetans are so kind and polite. They highly respect their elders, and when talking with them, the people are always polite and modest. The most interesting is that in Tibet, no matter what kind of day it may be and what kind of scene may be playing out, people love to wear their traditional clothing. By contrast, in my home country, only on a few special days, like our national day, do we see people do their traditional attire." Jessica then becomes resolute and says, "We must preserve our unique traditional culture and not lose it. It is our roots that provide US with the 'nutrients' to be who we are today. Inheriting and developing traditional culture is our responsibility; we must not be hesitant about this! If, in the future, we can still find our roots driving us forward, that will be a very happy day, indeed!"

When she is done with her studies, Jessica plans to stay in Lhasa and find a job. I smile and look at her blue eyes, and l wonder if the blue color is the same as her native seas or that of the blue Tibetan sky?

Like Pema Metok, Pasang and Yeshe Tsomo, there are several groups of foreign students studying Tibetan in the Tibet University, having graduated one class at a time, one after the other. Ever since the first group of students were enrolled in 1993, the Tibet University has adopted an open attitude in welcoming students from many countries, including the United States, Japan, Australia, New Zealand, the United Kingdom, and several others, totaling 500-odd students from over twenty countries, to study Tibetan. Along with language study, the university has also set up a culturally related curriculum for students to learn Tibetan music, arts, calligraphy, and many other facets of the local life. The school has also arranged for students to visit cultural sites, has invited experts to give lectures, and has set up diverse practice-based

Jessica takes a photo in the Longwangtan Park.

activities to provide as many opportunities as possible for students from all over the world to learn Tibetan and understand the people's culture. Attending foreign students can enjoy the exclusive life of the plateau as well as a new level of happiness brought to them through new doors opened from language study and precious cultural experiences. Their lives have become enriched, and their cultural exchanges and integrative activities have showered them with even more dreams that can now be shared and passed around the entire world.

Issue: No.5, 2017.

25
THE FIRST GROUP OF TIBETAN SAILORS

Text by Yan Enze

In May 2007, Lhosum Chophel and seven other Tibetans signed a contract with the Shanghai Shipping Transportation Company to formally join the company as sailors. Hence, the big family of China Shipping has its first group of Tibetan sailors.

The story dates back three years.

In 2004, the Shanghai Company sent a group of staff to support Tibet. They advanced the idea of recruiting Tibetan sailors, which was fully supported by the local government of Lholung County. In early August, 2005, parents brought their children from far away to make an application and hoped that their children would be successful so as to get chance to leave the mountain range and see what the world outside could offer.

Having gone through a general knowledge test and a physical examination, seven young Tibetans were finally enrolled.

On August 24th, 2005, the seven Tibetans traveled to Shanghai via Chengdu. When they arrived at the training centre, the faculty and students of over 50 welcomed them at the entrance of the training centre. Classmates helped them to their dormitory by carrying their luggage.

After four and a half months of the training program, the seven Tibetans received certificates and then joined another extensive training program for specific positions.

In June 2006, all of them were sent on a voyage for training. Lhosum was assigned to the ship Minhe. He was supported and encouraged by both the officers and crew on this ship. For instance, the captain assigned an experienced sailor to tutor him and his health and accommodation was also monitored in detail by the captain and the other officers. They sincerely hoped that all their efforts would result in Lhosum's quick adaptation to work and life on the ship. On June 7th, the ship sailed to Xinsha of Guangzhou. The captain took him for sightseeing tour of the city and tasted the local food. Like Lhosum Chophel, their colleagues cared for the other six Tibetan sailors, not only during their training program, but their living conditions as well.

Last spring, having gone through the whole procedure of evaluation and

In March, 2007, the reporter interviewed and had a group photo with the first group of Tibetan sailors.

the extensive, experimental on-the-job training program on ships, the seven Tibetan sailors successfully accomplished their training and went home for a holiday. I encountered them while I was conducting my interviews in Lholung County. These Tibetans' lives were changed and their employment, earning a fixed income, planted the idea of employment change amongst local herdsmen and farmers. They began to actively encourage their children to go to school.

The economic situation of the families of most of the seven sailors is poor. They have raised their yaks and sheep in a remote area and rarely gone outside. Some of them have only traveled as far as Lhasa. They are fond of sports, including football and basketball, and of course they are particularly fond of singing and dancing.

Lhosum Tsering, with a dark face but red checks, is the most active person amongst them. He was a singer on a one-year contract with a local *Langma* pub. He always says that it's better to do his best if people would choose him to do so.

Lhosum Tender is 1.74 metres high. He has a rather slim but long face. He looks very energetic. When he was seven to eight years old, he tended the family's livestock. Originally, he had dreamed of being a basketball player, but now he wishes to be a good sailor. Tenzin Nyima looks slim as well, but he loves to enjoy music and to swim. Although he did not realize his dream to visit Lhasa, he went to Shanghai, and he always feels excited because he believes he will go abroad. At present, he is working on the ship as technician. Dreaming to be a policeman, Lhosum Tenzin participated in the 2005 national university entrance examination. Unfortunately, a sports university rather than a police university accepted him. He gave up and finally became an international sailor for China.

Lhosum Chophel is the youngest amongst the seven, being born in 1987. He looks very gentle. He came to me to have this interview accompanied by his grandmother. He is an extremely good singer and always impressed his audience. While in his hometown, he took various jobs, such as labor worker. He has a very beautiful dream of his future career as a sailor and swears to do his best.

Tibetan sailors in class.

Choning Rachu is a mechanical technician. He looks slim too, but he has a really good family background. He in particular loved painting when he studied in middle school. His drawings usually feature people, birds and *Thangka*. He had dreamed of enrolling in art universities to study art. He said, as a sailor, he could also draw his pictures by viewing the sea and the landscape of other countries.

Jamyang Lodro graduated from a secondary computer technical school. He has a good physique. He had even dreamed of being a security officer in the past. He believes his professional field of computers will definitely advance the modernization of ships.

Having already left Lholung County over a year ago, Lhosum Chophel is still excited whenever he hears news from his hometown. It has been four months towards training to be a professional sailor. So thus we have followed the different routes of our seven Tibetans on their voyages in pursuit of being excellent Tibetan sailors.

Issue: No.1, 2008

26
NGAWANG NORBU'S DIARY
— A Record of a Special Mountaining Event

Text by Ngawang Norbu

Editor's Notes: On May 8th 2008, the Beijing Olympic torch relay team successfully reached the summit of Mt. Qomolangma.

About 9: 11 a.m, at a spot 30 meters from the peak, Lozang Dradul ignited the first torch that had been named "Auspicious Clouds" and was held by the female Tibetan mountaineer Jiji. Then, the torch was relayed to Wang Yongfeng, Nyima Tsering, Huang Chungui, and finally to another female Tibetan mountaineer Tsering Wangmo, who gave a final display of the now well-alight torch on the summit of Mt. Qomolangma.

The successful torch relay ceremony on the summit of Mt. Qomolangma was closed by the unfolding of the five-star flag of China, the flag of the Olympics, and also the Beijing 2008 Olympic flag. It was the historic moment at which China had fulfilled its solemn oath to the International Olympic Committee and also to the world, to take the torch relay to the summit of Mt. Qomolangma.

Ngawang Norbu, as this team's photographer, witnessed this success and recorded it all along. And further more, from his diary, we can get more and enjoy more.

March 25th, a day in which the weather was not too bad

Today the torch relay team, including mountaineers and photographers, set off from Lhasa to the base camp to climb Mt. Qomolangma. We had rushed to pack our luggage and were ready to go.

About two o'clock, we all met in the Tibetan Mountaineering School and the leaders of the Bureau of Sports came to wish us well. Arriving at Shigatse at six o'clock in the afternoon, we spent the night in the Holy Lake Hotels.

March 26th, a clear and sunny day

Having had our breakfast. we set off for Dingri County(Shekar). The 250-kilometer road was well made, having been upgraded last year. We easily reached Shekar by five o'clock in the afternoon. The weather was so favorable it was almost like in Lhasa. Having had dinner, most of us met casually in a local teashop. I met an old classmate of mine from our primary school years who was now teaching in Dingri Primary School. We had not seen each other since we both graduated from primary school. He looked Just the same, no change at all.

March 27th, a sunny day again

Last night I slept poorly. Maybe it was too cold as the hotel only provided one quilt for each bed. The weather was always cold at night.

We set out at 9:30 a.m. from Shekar for the base camp. On the way we passed through five checkpoints and were very strictly guarded. I believe this was necessary since the visit of the torch to Mt. Qomolangma was very important.

It was about two o'clock in the afternoon when we reached the base camp. The support team had successfully accomplished all logistical preparations for us. They had already erected 50 tents. To clear a path beyond the 6500-meter elevation was the first of today's tasks and they had already prepared a path from 6,500 to 7,028 meters.

March 29th, a windy day

After breakfast, we had a meeting. Many key leaders participated, including Nyinma (Principal of Tibetan Mountaineering School), Wang Yongfeng (team leader of the National Mountaineering Contingent), Luo Shen (coach of the National Mountaineering Contingent), and Zhang Jianyuan (the team leader of China Mountaineering Association). The meeting discussed how tomorrow we would climb to a higher point by clearing the path and organizing the transportation of our supplies and equipment. Finally we were divided into three groups to complete this task. As usual, this task was given to the team from the Tibetan Mountaineering School.

April 1st, a sunny day

Light snow fell at the base camp last night, but the weather this morning was wonderful.

At this time we were overloaded with tasks, mainly focusing on erecting the tents. Though fifteen of our team members were photographers and reasonably experienced with mountaineering, the physical strain of recent days made us a little afraid of the coming physical challenge of the torch relay.

April 4th, again another nice and sunny day

We were still erecting tents and almost worn out.

April 5th, a cloudy day

It was a cloudy day but not windy, and not as cold as the previous two days.

The two tents for the television live broadcast were erected as well as another two tents to serve as a temporary restaurant; one for Chinese cuisine and the other for Tibetan. The later was also used for various activities during the relay event.

April 6th, snowing

When we got up in the morning, the outside of the tent was already covered with snow. Obviously it had snowed during the night but not heavily—the first snow since we got here. The weather was fine in the morning, but gradually it turned cold during the afternoon.

The path has already been cleared to 7,790 meters above sea level. The weather in the last two days did set us some hurdles to clear while clearing the path. Dratse phoned to tell me that they would begin bringing our supplies tomorrow. Several of us were still working on erecting the tents and had no time to help them. We had to rely mainly on the hired laborers; otherwise, it would be impossible to get everything done.

April 8th, a sunny day

I heard over a hundred people were going to arrive at the camp tomorrow. This year would be an historic one for the base camp of Mt. Qomolangma to host so many people.

April 12th, again another sunny day

I had an awful sleep last night at our camp, 5,800 meters above sea level. Though I did not get a headache, I could not sleep until very early in the morning. I tried to lie in bed a little longer when the morning came but the person in charge of the yaks called me. He wanted to get back the cushion I had borrowed to sleep on last night and which was originally brought from the base camp by yak. I had to raise my heavy body, pack everything and hand it over to the person who was going to take care of it. Today. in the land of 5,800 meters above sea level, the weather was really favorable. There was no wind. Compared with previous meals, the food here was unsatisfying. Apart from instant noodles, only *Tsampa* was available. Most of us dislike instant noodles. Having eaten a little bit of *Tsampa*, we set off on our journey. This was our first time to walk toward the camps where the torch relay would begin, referred as to the "progressing camps" We tried to keep up a brisk pace in order to maintain our physical strength and avoid headaches.

When we reached the 6,000-meter level, we met the main group of team members walking down to the base camp for a brief rest. They have been clearing a path to the 8,300-meter level and had successfully transported supplies to the temporary progressing camp at 7,790 meters. According to the weather forecast, the weather conditions will deteriorate within 18 days. By and large, this was a good opportunity to have them come down to the base camp. At 6,000 meters it was snowing. The camp for the beginning of the torch relay was just 100 meters away from the international camp. Having had our lunch, we began setting up tents for ourselves.

April 14th, a sunny day

We were asked to carry supplies from Camp 1 at 7,028 meters above sea level, and another 20 team members were sent to take supplies to Camp 2 at 7,790 meter above sea level. Those going to Camp 2 were asked to set off at six o'clock in the morning, but we could wait until 10:30 a.m. We took the responsibility to carry the oxygen supply tanks and the ropes used along the pathway. Though some team members. Whom we met coming down. told US of the challenge ahead of us in walking up the north face of Mt. Qomolangma, mainly because of severely icy conditions. I felt it was not too bad in comparison with the conditions I encountered last year. Maybe it was due to the snow over the last two days that made movement a little bit difficult. But I did have an easy journey today. At about 3 p.m., we arrived at Camp 1.

April 19-24th, the weather was not too bad

I had developed a slight toothache since last night. In the afternoon it seemed to be much worse. I was annoyed because I did not want to jeopardize my chance to get to the summit of Mt. Qomolangma. I went to the clinic to have an injection while absenting myself from my duties.

After two days I had not really recovered from my toothache, while the other team members had moved to another progressing camp. I had more injections. Since the other team members had all climbed up to another camp I really had nothing to do in those two days. I wish my toothache would get better soon.

April 25th, a sunny day

I am better today and plan to reach 6,500 meters above sea level.

April 28th, a windy day

The weather in the region of Mt. Qomolangma has completely changed. Since April 25th , the wind has dramatically increased and it got much worse at night. We were afraid the tents would blow away. Fortunately, the wind tended to drop after we woke in the morning.

The bad weather continued. We had to keep our fingers crossed for favorable weather while waiting in the camp at 6,500 meters. Time was running out but chere was nothing we could do and só we were very worried.

April 30th, another very windy day

Today is 100 days to the opening ceremony of the Beijing Olympic Games. The China Central Television (CCTV) conducted its first live broadcast from Mt. Qomolangma, which lasted about one and half hours, to show the preparations for the torch relay and the camp at 6,500 meters. We, and several mountaineering photographers, also had a part in the live broadcast.

Currently, since over 100 persons are staying at the 6,500-meter camp, the caterers are running around like headless chickens.

By noon, the torches and flame had arrived at the camp and were handed over to the team leader of our group.

May 1st, the weather is not too bad

Today is National Labor Day. In fact, we had almost forgotten about festivals in recent months since we had been on the mountains. Worse still, many of us even obliterated all memory of specific dates. To us, there was no point to keep track of dates. Rather, we only wished the weather could improve so that we could shorten the time taken to climb the mountain. However, these two days of bad weather really bothered us and we were, to some extent, discouraged. We worried about it a lot, and desperately wished the weather would change so that we could quickly finish our tasks.

After dinner, I went to the activity tent and picked up a book to read. Mr. Geng from CCTV pulled me out of the tent and told me the good news; I had been selected as one of the torchbearers from the base camp. I was originally recruited as a mountaineering photographer for this journey and I did not expect to be part of the show. It was a big surprise and very exciting.

May 2nd, the weather is not too bad

The weather looked very good in the morning. We all looked forward to nice weather for the coming days, but things are sometimes not what you dreamed. For a while in the morning, wind started to blow hard and it became even colder than the previous two days. Again, we had to take shelter at the 6,500-meter camp and wait for the weather to improve.

By noon, four local employees backpacked dumplings from the base camp. The chance to have a taste of delicious dumplings cheered us up considerably. Since there were too many people in this camp, we had to queue in a lengthy line to get our dumplings. After everybody had filled his or her stomachs, we were called to a meeting. The commander-in-chief of the relay, Mr. Wang, the Principal Nyima and the coach Mr. Luo, all joined us to decide who would take charge of transportation of supplies to the camp at 8300 meters for tomorrow.

May 3rd, weather still not too bad

Waking up in the morning. I saw snow had covered the ground. It must have snowed last night. The team in charge of transportation to the camp at 8300 meters had already set out around four or five o'clock in the morning. I guessed they must be exhausted since the snow did not stop. Fortunately, they were not troubled by any wind.

Tomorrow, eight students from my mountaineering school will work with three mountaineers from the Tibetan Mountaineering Team to clear a path to reach 7,790 meters above sea level. The current plan is to make a path to reach the summit within three days.

The team of mountaineering photographers had a slight change in function. The photographer in fourth position and the technician in charge of microwave technology were both asked to clear the path. I had to urgently discuss this personnel change with Dratse to make it possible for Tashi Phuntshogs to replace Tsering Tendar so that we could ensure at least one of photographers could have the opportunity to reach the summit of Mt. Qomolangma.

May 4th, the weather is not too bad

The team for clearing the path was sent out for further work along the route of the torch relay, even though it was still snowing. Fortunately, the weather forecast predicted that it was going to be nice weather as of today. But we did feel there wasn't a big change in Nature's compassion for us regarding the weather during these two days. Therefore, the team did not set off on time, according to the previous schedule, but waited instead for the order from the base camp. At 10 o'clock that order came. Since the order was a little late and we might not reach Camp 2 (7,790 meter above sea level) in time, the team decided to postpone their agenda to the next day.

Today, the torches and flame were sent to the camps furthest from base camp. Usually we took two days from the base camp to the first progressing camp. But today the group only took one day to reach it. They must be worn out! About six o'clock, on hearing the bodyguard for the contingent carrying the torches and flame was coming; we burst out of the tents to greet them. They were really exhausted.

May 5th, a sunny day

Today the weather is favorable. At 9 a.m., eleven members of the team set out to clear the path. At 10 a.m., we collected our photographic equipment from the technological supply department of CCTV. The equipment was bigger than usual and also much heavier. Our mountaineering photographers were divided into teams of two persons. Each of us has to load up with 6 kilograms of equipment. Therefore, the total load was actually 20 kilograms per individual, as we each had to carry our own stuff as well. At 11 a.m., the torch relay ceremony began.

Norbu Dradul and Phurbu Dondrup began the torch relay. They set off in advance of the others after the torch was handed to them. The others would set out by 3 p.m. On having lunched and taken a short rest we started to climb the mountain. Before setting out, the people who were staying at the progressing camp, including the logistical, said farewell and blessed us. They wished us success in reaching the summit. On the way, it was hot because we had already put on our velvet clothes and trousers to reduce our load.

When we got Camp 1 (7,028 meters above sea level) it was already 6 o'clock. The selection for this team was actually a very good match. We constantly photographed and tried to catch every significant moment in the whole procession. Even though it was, to some extent, very we managed well and climbed at a brisk pace.

May 6th, the weather is not too bad

According to the plan, we had to set off at 10 a.m. from the 7028-meters camp to Camp 2 (7,790 meters above sea level). No doubt, this is the longest distance between camps. On hearing that they were low on oxygen supply bottles at Camp 2, we were asked to carry one each. There fore we, the photographers, were more overloaded.

The weather was not perfect as it was windy. It was difficult to move forward. We arrived at Camp 2 about 3 p.m. and started to erect tents. The wind at Camp 2 was so severe it took us a long time to set up a tent. The oxygen bottles that we had carried could now enable us to have a good sleep during the night and we felt rejuvenated the next morning.

May 7th, a sunny day

It seemed a nice day when we got up. This was the weather all of us had hoped for. We were going to leave at 11 a.m.

I had an interview with the organizers of this event, Principal Nyima and Mr. Wang, in the morning. Just before setting off, the team clearing the path brought us good news: they had already successfully cleared the path to the summit. When we all were ready, we set off toward today's destination-the camp at 8,300 meters above sea level, which was actually the last camp before the summit. If we could climb quickly enough from 7,790 meters to 8,300 meters, we could get there in three to four hours. When we reached about 8,200 meters above sea level, the team clearing the path retreated from the summit. They were descending quickly and planed to reach the 6,500-meter camp today.

Having arrived at the 8,300-meter camp we did not stop to draw breath but immediately set up the tents. This was actually quite challenging, particularly at such high altitudes and such an uneven surface, though the land was not covered by snow. Each tent could accommodate three to four persons. After this, we were up to our eyeballs in the preparation of our equipment. We communicated with the base camp by radio. At first, the radio was unsatisfactory, but it became perfect after adjustment by technicians in the base camp. We checked and adjusted each of the four microwave dishes and transferred all the pictures we took on the way to the different progressing camps. When everything was done, I was asked to have a meeting with the Principal Nyima and the team leader Mr. Wang. They imparted to me the plan for climbing to the summit tomorrow. We divided people into three groups. One group is to be in charge of bodyguards of the torch, setting out at 2 a.m. The second group is our mountaineering photographers, also leaving at 2 a.m. The last one is the torch relay group, setting out at 3 a.m.

I gobbled some food. In general, at such high altitudes, we are used to not having much food. Since tomorrow is to be a challenging day I have to go to bed early.

May 8th, a sunny day

I did not sleep well yesterday since we had only three sleeping bags for four persons. The night was cold. About one o'clock in the morning, I thought I heard somebody calling my name. I got up and peeked outside. It was Mr. Wang, the team leader. He asked me to get ready to set off. I rushed to dress and tried to boil some snowmelt water. The portable cooker was very small and took ages to boil the water. Finally, about 3 o'clock in the morning. we set out. The weather was very calm. There was no wind. The whole procession progressed at a furious pace. We originally planned to begin the live broadcast when we reached the first high camp but when we got there it was just six o'clock in the morning and still dark. We could do nothing without sufficient light, so the base camp decided to cancel the live broadcast at the second highest level. Notwithstanding, I continued to do my best to record all that happened at these two highest levels in the hope that maybe sometime in the future, I might have the opportunity to send out these pictures to the public.

Wangdu took out his camera to begin shooting but unfortunately, the connection between his camera and battery was broken. Maybe it was the cold weather which froze the line and made it too fragile. This was our first encounter with trouble but it made us nervous. If the other lines failed how could we succeed with the live broadcast? So we transferred the cables from the camera box into the packets of velvet clothes in order to keep them warm.

The whole procession walked on very fast. If we kept walking at this rate we could probably reach the summit before the sunrise. As a consequence of this, we might not be able to conduct a live broadcast because of insufficient light. Therefore, when we reached the third highest level, the two commanders—Nyima and Mr. Wang—asked us to reduce our pace. We stayed another half an hour at the third highest base until the sky began to lighten. The first live broadcast started at the 8,800-meter level, half an hour's walk from the summit. Three cameras were installed at the summit. The first one was only 30 meters below the 8,844-meter level-the summit.

It was about 9 o'clock in the morning of May 8th, 2008 when the Beijing Olympics torch flame was ignited near the summit of Mt. Qomolangma. The first torchbearer in this 1ast relay to the summit of Mt. Qomolangma was Jiji, the female Tibetan mountaineer. She raised the torch high on the summit. The second camera caught the moment of the relay of the torch from Jiji to Mr. Wang Yongfeng and then to Nyima. My camera was installed at the peak of the summit to shoot the torch relay to the fourth carrier Agui, the university students'representative. In addition, from my position I could also catch the activities of another torch carder, Tsering Wangmo.

In this event, the people involved were four bodyguards of the torches from the China Mountaineering Team, eight mountaineering photographers, 12 torch carriers, and seven volunteers. Twenty-two of the total thirty-one participants were from the Tibetan Mountaineering School. We have successfully recorded the entire progress of the torch relay to the summit of Mt. Qomolangma, including the moment when mountaineers of China raised the Chinese national flag, the flag of the 2008 Beijing Olympic Games, and the flag of the five rings of the Olympics. This is an invaluable record to show the world the moment and the scene when the torch flame of the 2008 Beijing Olympic Games was ignited at the summit of the highest spot on Earth. At this moment we were all very excited. This is the dream of our people. As Chinese citizens, we are proud of our country, and we cheered that our dream had become reality. All team members shouted in unison: "One world, one dream".

We stayed at the summit for about one hour. The weather there was not pleasant, being shrouded with fog and battered by a strong wind. Of course, It was also very cold. Our hands felt numb since we had to work for a long. period with our hands. We started to descend about 10:40 a.m. As is known universally. climbing up a mountain is always easier than descending. Since everybody was so exhausted. we walked down at a very slow pace. When we got to the camp at the 8,300-meter level, the logistics staff prepared hot water and food for us. Gradually. one by one, everybody arrived at the camp and some even kept on moving further down. People with different levels of physical strength showed correspondingly different rates of descent from the mountain. But all of us had been asked to reach the camp at 6,500 meters. It was already five o'clock in the afternoon. Most of our team members were still behind us. Some of them might only reach the camp at 10 o'clock at night.

Issue: No.5, 2008.

27

AFFECTIONS GROW IN THE SNOW-COVERED LAND

— A Story of Three Tibetan Mothers Working as Mail Carriers for 27 Years for the Soldiers at Frontier Outposts

Text & Photo by Ya Tongbing

On the south wing of the Himalayas, a mountain lies at an elevation of 4000 meters. Unattractive frontier outposts located on the mountainside closely connect with three Tibetan women. They are from Rinchengung Village in Dromo (Yadong) County of Tibet; their names are Dekyi, Tsering Chodron, and Butri. The stories regarding their support for soldiers over 27 years are widely spread and eulogized.

On their own initiative, from the early 1980s these three matriarchs began to provide vegetables for the outposts. In winter they would visit once a week, but in summer twice a week. For 27 years, their journey to provide this service for the outposts reached 5,000 kilometers. providing of a total of 6,500 kilograms of vegetables and delivering 50,000 mail items. Their round trips to the outposts totaled 50,000 kilometers. Soldiers fondly referred to them as “A Ma”(Tibetan, meaning “dear mother”).

Carrying Vegetables While Delivering Mail

It was quite common in winter that soldiers quartering in the frontier

Butri (left), Tsering Chodron (right) and Dekyi (right second) pictured together with a soldier in the border outpost.

outposts of Domkhar Lha, Tralangse, Tseli Lha, Doring and Drolha, could only get the "three typical substances": agaric, bean vermicelli, and cans of various kinds. Obviously, vegetables were luxury items for them. One year Ridro, a matriarch, had already been in the area for about 40 years, was concerned that she could not continue the provision of vegetables as her arthritis had become much worse. Therefore, the following year she brought Dekyi with her. On Dekyi's first visit to the outpost with Ridro she was deeply impressed. She said with emotion: "I could hardly image how these soldiers who had come to Tibet to emancipate us, were living in such terrible conditions!" She observed: "Ridro and I came to provide vegetables to the soldiers for about three years. During that particular period, the road conditions were awful. Later, Ridro's legs could not carry her anymore. Henceforth, I took Butri and Tsering Chodron to continue providing that

While veterans are about to leave, the mothers come to farewell their "sons".

service to the soldiers. Sometimes, it was just one of us, other times two or three of us."

From then on, in the small village people would frequently see the three "mothers" set out at dawn to trek to the outposts to provide vegetables to the soldiers. Often, they delivered once or twice a week. This continued for 27 years. Today, Dekyi who was a 26-year-girl on her first journey to provide service to the outposts has become a mature woman.

From 1982, Dekyi has never halted her service to the outposts by providing vegetables and delivering mail for soldiers, no matter how busy she was on her farm, even though the round trip to the outposts is about 50 kilometers and took many hours on the way.

"One day in August 1995, as usual, I was carrying my backpack of vegetables to the outpost. As I passed through a dense forest, I sang a folk song to myself so that I would not feel alone. But close to the forest, I suddenly saw a black bear staring at me from a short distance. I could not move and dared not shout for help, but I wanted to cry. The stand off for about tens minutes, I lifted my voice to sing another song in order to encourage myself. Unbelievably, the bear was terrified and ran away. Whenever I remember the incident. I still feel afraid." said Dekyi with a big smile.

Whenever these ladies went to the outposts they always brought the mail of soldiers since the outposts are isolated and located in remote areas without any access to transport. It is common that one letter from inland China can take at least one month to reach the soldiers' hands. Sometimes, half a year is not unusual. Therefore, the soldiers decided to give Dekyi's address to their families so that in every case the could personally bring all soldiers' mail to the outpost. Eventually, she became the mail carrier for all the soldiers living in the outposts.

"Once, Dekyi was carrying over 25 kilograms of vegetables across the snow covered pass of Mt. Dungkar, which was 4,300 meters above sea level. All a sudden, the sky turned dark and she was cau2ht in a blizzard. She was almost completely covered by the merciless snow and could hardly move because of the heavy weight of the vegetables and the snow that blocked her way. She fell in the snow several times and struggled to walk about 200 meters. In the gloom, she saw a cave where she thought she could escape from the blizzard for a while. So she struggled to drag herself into the cave and stayed there for about five hours. On the following day, when she appeared in front of the outpost, almost all the soldiers burst into tears of joy while they hugged the "yeti-1ike" Mother Dekyi. She, however, just smiled when she saw her many "sons".

The spring festival was coming in 2001; Dekyi was preparing to deliver vegetables to the outpost situated at Tralangse. Unfortunately, the snow was extremely heavy, almost reaching to her knee. Dekyi could not continue in such icy snow since she had to climb instead of walk. She finally fell down and her legs felt completely numb. She had to pass all the vegetables to Butri to keep on delivering them to the soldiers.

Love Knots Tied Deep Their Hearts

Whenever questioned why they keep on delivering vegetables to those soldiers, these women answer, "I am the little Pumo (Tibetan, meaning 'little girl') grown up in the arms of the uncles and aunts from People's Liberation Army. The statue of Chairman Mao Zedong, the red five-star flag and the red shoulder ornament are all my memo of my childhood. "

In 1954, the PLA came to reside in Dromo County. No matter whether soldiers or their commanders, they all lived with civilians while they were working with them on their farms, on disaster relief, and transporting ammunition. During that particular period, the parents of Dekyi had built a profound friendship with PLA soldiers. Her father, Panpa Tsering, even joined the militia for about eight years. Amongst the three women, the families of Tsering Chodron and Dekyi were previously the serfs of local landlords. Atier the democratic reform had taken place in Tibet. they changed their social status to assume their own lives and freedom. They were given land and flocks. In 1978, Tsering Chodron won the first prize of the militia competition in the Military Area of Chengdu. Her husband Tenzin was recruited by the PLA in 1981 and gave five years of service in the military force as a team leader.

Mutual assistance between the soldiers and the local people is quite a common phenomenon. Once, Dekyi suffered from acute pain. On hearing this news, the commander of the PLA immediately sent a physician of internal medicine and two nurses to see Dekyi. In that moment, Dekyi's face turned pale and she could hardly draw a breath. Finally she fainted. Without hesitation, the doctor sent her to the medical department of the military force to have surgery. Two hours later Dekyi's life was saved. Thereafter Dekyi appreciated her rescue by the PLA and started, by various actions, to pay them back.

Whenever soldiers caught flu, she brought medicine to them. The three women treated the soldiers just like their sons. Sometimes when soldiers came back from their vacation. they would visit the families of the three women as though they were the soldiers' families. In December of 2004,

Dekyi and Butri on their way to deliver vegetables.

the wife and child of the lieutenant came to visit him. The snow had sealed off the mountain pass and they could not access the outpost. The visitors panicked. On hearing this, Dekyi, took the visitors to her house in the downtown of the county and treated them to buttered tea, eggs and fresh yak meat to give them sufficient nutrition to cope with high altitude sickness.

In March 2007, the outpost situated at Tralangse was hit by a big avalanche and three young soldiers lost their lives. The three women, on hearing this news, were running about and sobbing. They could not eat or sleep as if they had lost their own "sons". They brought out *khada* and incense to express their condolences by following their traditional funeral customs.

When Lu Yunhua, a solider from Zhejiang Province, retired from the army, he left his photo to the women with the inscription "A Ma La" (Tibetan, meaning "My dear mother"), we have shared a wonderful life with you. I am going to be discharged from military service soon, but please don't be sad. Whenever you miss me, you could take a look at my photo and I will bless you from far away. "To date, the three women have at least 500 letters from retired soldiers. They treat those letters carefully, just like their treasures." Dekyi said: "I felt so happy and relieved when I received letters from those veterans, as I did when I ensured vegetables were available to the soldiers while they could receive their mail."

The three women's disinterested devotion from year to year has been an example to others in the village. These days, more and more villagers have joined this team to provide support for the soldiers. The village organizes a special delivery team using mules for transport to deliver vegetables to the soldiers living in the outposts.

The Tibetan Mothers Are Soldiers' Own Mothers

The maternal affection between the three women and the soldiers has been firmly established through the delivery of vegetables and mail. These three have now reached mature ages: 56 (Degyi), 53 (Tsering Chodron) and 48 (Butri) respectively. They take care of the soldiers just like their own sons in many aspects; in return, the soldiers look after the three mothers as if they were their own birth mothers. Tsering Chodron said: "I had a feeling of that these soldier-sons shared a special Karma with me. It seems it is my fate. Whenever I saw them, I felt that they were all my sons. After not seeing them for several day, my hearts feels empty and I worry about them so much".

Wen Junjie, the deputy lieutenant, observed: "When these women come to deliver vegetables, I do feel they are my mothers. I have no way to repay them. What I can do is to do the best job I can to safeguard the territory of the motherland." Tashi, the deputy commander, said: "Our soldiers are just like the family members of these three women. All those retired soldiers want to leave their addresses with their adopted mothers, and after they returned to home they often phone them to share their happy lives with them, such as telling them about their new lives in their hometown, their employment

The mothers and soldiers have all passed along this road for tens years in the highland.

situation, marriage situation, and information about their children, all kinds of news and happiness."

Whenever the busy farming season comes, the army likes to organize soldiers to help the women gather crops in the field. Whenever possible, the

Whenever festivals come, including Tibetan New year, the local soldiers go out of their way to see the three mothers, and invite them to join their festival celebration.

soldiers also provide help carrying water, chopping firewood, washing quilts, providing medical services, teaching about planting technology and breeding skills. Soldiers are constantly retiring and being replaced with newcomers but the culture of mutual help does not change. The soldiers always treat the women as their mothers and share their happiness and sadness with them. Whenever soldiers return from vacation, they all like to visit their adopted mothers with gifts of their hometown's specialties and to share news about their hometowns. This spring, the rainfall was surprisingly light. On one hand, for sake of help these women, the army sent over 100 soldiers several times to help them with farm labor such as carrying electricity generators and irrigation machines in order to minimize the economic loss to the women's families. On the other hand, the women tried to ask help from the soldiers as little as possible, though the soldiers constantly asked them what they can do for them to help with their difficulties.

Apart from sending vegetables and delivering mail to the soldiers, these mothers voluntarily take the role of Tibetan teachers for the soldiers. Every time, they set out at four o'clock in the morning and trek for over twelve hours for the round trip to visit the soldiers. They teach the soldiers for several hours in Tibetan oral language. When they get back home, it is always already ten o'clock in the night. One of soldiers said passionately: "The Tibetan we have learnt from these women has helped us tremendously in fulfilling our duties here." In addition. the mothers pass on local cultural knowledge to the soldiers while they are teaching language. Alternately, a veteran from Guangdong runs a Tibetan shop in his hometown selling Tibetan accessories while telling his customers the function and uses of those Tibetan accessories. His rich cultural experience was learnt from the three women and has resulted in a booming business. With deep affection, he says, " These women not only provided the military force with great assistance, but are also excellent tutors for our individual soldiers." Similarly, another soldier who is from Hangzhou of Zhejiang learnt Tibetan cooking skills from the women, and his recent retirement enables him to ran a Tibetan restaurant in Lake Xihu in Hangzhou, a famous tourist attraction. His business is prosperous and he always keeps in contact with these women.

Tashi Delek! A Ma La

On every Army Festival on August 1st, New Year, Spring Festival and Tibetan New Year, the army takes fruit, flour, cans and white sugar to visit the three women, lead by the leadership of the army. In the meanwhile, they are invited to participate in the festival gatherings with soldiers.

On the last day of 2008, the three women were invited to celebrate the New Year with soldiers. When the soldiers saw them, they were pleased and excited. They surrounded the women, asking how they were. The deputy lieutenant, Phurjung Da, said to the three women "A Ma La, thanks for all that you have done for us by sending us vegetables without any break for so many years. Your contribution changed our lives as soldiers. We are deeply grateful. Here I would like, on behalf of every soldier, to express our heartfelt appreciation to you! We sincerely wish You three would have a happy New Year and *Tashi Delek* (Tibetan, meaning 'blessings, auspicious signs and good luck')." On saying that, he solemnly saluted the three women and then presented *khada* (a white silk scarf) to them in gratitude. The soldiers sat in a circle around them and presented them with all kinds of dishes. It seemed like a real family moment with their real mothers. Everyone was cheerful and in high spirits.

Currently, with policies aiming to increase the prosperity of the people and the assistance from the resident soldiers, the three women's livelihood has undergone an earthshaking change. The families of Dekyi and Tsering Chordron have already built their spacious Tibetan house. In 2006, universities enrolled Dekyi's three daughters but with economic constraints, the family could barely afford the tuition fees. On heating this, the soldiers voluntarily donated cash to Dekyi for her daughters. When Dekyi refused, the soldiers said: "Please take it because we are all your sons and we don't like our siblings to drop out from universities." Henceforth, in every semester, the three daughters always receive the supporting cash for their tuition. At present, the eldest daughter has already graduated from university and become a teacher. The second daughter is studying in the Teachers' University of Shanxi, and the youngest daughter is soon going to graduate from Lhasa Commercial and Business School.

Issue: No.6, 2009.

28
A TIBETAN CHINESE COUPLE'S GOLDEN MARRIAGE

Text by Liu Hongming

"My colleague said to me, 'Why not get divorced? He is bound to be disabled,' but I did not do it. I could not do it with a Tibetan conscience." Tsering Sonam, the 75-year-old Ama, said indifferently as she recalled the scene from 44 years ago.

This is a story about this old Tibetan woman and her Chinese husband, Zhang Huaxiang. Hand in hand, they have lived together for 50 years. Tsering Sonam's husband only has one knuckle left on each finger and only four fingers on his left hand due to tendon ruptures. After many cosmetic surgeries, though, his face and lips keep burning in scars. Their two children have never seen their father's real countenance ever since they were born.

Time may weather memories, but true love becomes fresher as time goes on, regardless of region and nationality.

About 50 years ago, Zhang Huaxiang, a man from Sichuan, was assigned to work in Namling County, Tibet. He was introduced to Tsering Sonam, and soon, their love for each other began to blossom. In the summer of 1962, the two of them received a marriage license at Namling County.

"Though I am Tibetan, he is Chinese. Still, I find no difference between us," Tsering Sonam said when talking of her impression of Zhang Huaxiang during those years. "He is handsome, simple, reliable, and good at

Tsering Sonam and Zhang Huaxiang take a photo with their granddaughters.

everything."

"She wears long braids and casual clothes, talking little and being somewhat shy," Zhang Huaxiang said when asked about his impressions.

Their journey of marriage, however, did not go as smoothly as expected. It was not long before sudden disaster would fall upon the unsuspecting couple.

In 1970, spring was drier than usual in Tibet. A fire broke out on Mt. Nishe, Nyingchi Prefecture in February. At that time, Zhang Huaxiang was in the middle of his training in the area and went to put out the fire. The ruthless flames destroyed his countenance and broke off his ten fingers.

"At one moment, a gust rose suddenly, and we, dozens of people, who were putting out the fire together, were surrounded by wild flames all at once. We rolled down into the valley, and I was fortunately blocked by a pine. As I woke up, I found fire all around me, and the skin on my face and hands was all burned up," the 86-year-old recalled.

Since Tsering Sonam was pregnant that year, the local cadre concealed the news. She was not told that her husband was undergoing treatment in Shanghai until after their son had already become a few months old.

Upon hearing the news, the newly wedded wife did not accept the advice she received from her colleagues and friends. Though she and Zhang Huaxiang spent more time apart than they did together due to problems getting along before and after the wedding, her feelings for her husband and her family did not abate a bit, much less fade out just for the simple reason that he got wounded and would become disabled.

On the one hand, Tsering Sonam had to bring up her son and take care of her blind mother, but on the other hand, she had to shoulder her family's burdens and go to work in the villages. Meanwhile, Zhang Huaxiang went under the knife over twenty times and suffered great pain from large areas of skin grafting, the amputation of both hands, and the wire puncturing of two new hands that a normal person cannot bear. In many ways, he is no less than resurrected.

In the spring of 1973, Tsering Sonam came to Shanghai from the snow mountain with her two-year-old son. "I was so sad when I was told that he was burned so badly, but little did I know how serious this was. I told myself that no matter how bad it might become, I had to hold on. I had to do him good for the rest of his life since he was whom I chose. I would let my conscience down if I got divorced just because he was hurt like that," she said. "Love despises no nationality; everyone is common."

Tsering Sonam said, after trying to protect the property of the state, her husband was deemed a hero. His wounds are really a glorious honor, and in her heart, he was still that plain, talented, and handsome Chinese man that she always knew.

After a long four-year treatment, Zhang Huaxiang was able to recover and left the hospital in 1974. A long term recuperation period was arranged for him in Chengdu, during which Tsering Sonam was by his side at all times. For always having lived on the highlands, she actually never got used to the climate in Chengdu, but for her husband's health, she bore this in silence.

Zhang Huaxiang often told his friends and relatives, "Times were sweet during those years when I was in the hospital. Without my better half looking after me, I would have become ashes long before."

Zhou Dunyou, Zhang Huaxiang's fellow villager, college classmate, and colleague who graduated from the Buddhist College of China and was assigned to work in Tibet at the same year with Zhang in 1959, said, "Zhang Huaxiang had been very handsome, and I was shocked and could not recognize him when I saw him again. In 1975, I happened to have an opportunity to go on a business trip to Chengdu, so I went to see him. We gave each other a big hug the moment we met. Then, we were too excited to speak. We all shed tears." Zhou Dunyou, 86 years old, could not help his quavering voice as he recalled the reunion 40 years ago.

Phoenix Nirvana, a new lease on life! As a man who became disabled for the state, surely he could accept the arrangement of his organization to stay in Chengdu as long as he wanted and would not need to go into Tibet again. However, Zhang Huaxiang requested many times and finally was approved to return to Lhasa in 1980.

"After coming back to Lhasa, Zhang Huaxiang stuck to his work, though he suffered from altitude stress. He even was able to write with a pen! We all admired his strong mental attitude," Zhou Dunyou said. "Tsering Sonam is a great woman, too; to take care of her husband, she sacrificed her own career. If not for this situation, she may have taken more of a leading position a long time before."

The way Zhang Huaxiang looks is often talked about by many. Some people even said to Tsering Sonam to her face that her husband was downright scary. "It is none of your business whether he is scary or not," she retorted angrily. "He doesn't live with you! I don't worry about it, so what are you so worried about?!" After mentioning that, the old woman said slowly, "I later learned to let it go. It's natural that people feel uncomfortable when seeing him as they have never seen something like that before."

"Once upon a time, my better half went out for a haircut," Tsering Sonam said. "He went into a few barber shops, but nobody would serve him. His pride took a serious blow, and he would not go to any barber ever again."

So, for many years now, the woman has been giving her husband haircuts and has become very skilled at it.

Not only with a happy family, Zhang Huaxiang also has a group of Chinese and Tibetan friends who work together with him.

"Zhang is very generous; he has no friction with anyone. When someone came angrily one time and brought up an issue with salary, he was very patient in the way he came across," Nache, a colleague, said to this reporter.

Zhang Huaxing and Tsering Sonam.

Now, one of the two is over seventy years of age, with the other over eighty. The love and confidence between the Chinese and Tibetans help the elderly couple live across the chains of snowy mountains and beyond regions and nationalities in their lives.

"Tibet is continuing to develop more and more, and we don't worry about food and amusement anymore. Our biggest wish is to keep healthy and enjoy the life of today," the old couple said.

50 years of marriage is truly golden. 50 years of standing together through storm and stress has already tightly fused the two hearts of different nationalities. Their marriage has expanded across half a century, like a long string of gold that is hard to break.

"From my father and mother, I understand what inseparable love is and what a strong will, burden, and responsibility of a family can be," Tseyang, their daughter, said. "No matter what nationality you are, the dream to pursue one's happiness is always the same."

Issue: No.4, 2015.

29

NGAWANG, THE GUARDIAN OF THE TUNGGAR GROTTOS

Text by Chen Jianxin Photo by Cheng Demei

The ruins of Guge Kingdom in Zanda County, Ngari Prefecture include the Toling Monastery as well as the biggest soil forest within this world-famous tourist attraction. Still, few people know that there is a small village named Tunggar there in the small valley of Ngayi Lhari Mountain located 70 kilometers away from Zanda County. On the high-rise sandy cliffs near the village, there are many grottos with exquisite frescos inside them. In nearby Piyang Village, there is a large cultural relic site consisting of temples, castles, grottos, and pagodas. Built in the 10th Century A.D. during the reign of Rinchen Zangpo of the Guge Kingdom, these ruins all belong to a major monastery, which was an important cultural center of Guge.

Tunggar is a tiny village with only a dozen families. Many grottos are scattered on the bluff extending for over one kilometer to the north of the village, and the frescos within two of these grottos are especially striking.

Like the Guge relics, how and when the Tunggar grottos were formed could not be found in any Tibetan historical, religious, or cultural record. The ancient frescos here are precise in composition and vivid in their depiction of a variety of subjects featuring smooth lines, bright colors, and unique shapes including some exotic human figures, patterns, and shapes.

Ngawang has been guarding the Tunggar grotto relics for over 30 year.

The special mineral pigments used here have kept the colors fresh and non-faded for almost one thousand years. The main subjects of the frescos are Buddha, Bodhisattva, guardian deities, warriors, and sacrifice providers. The huge amount of mandala paintings is breathtaking. Those depicting Buddha's life, his preaching, and his worship are all original and creative, while the decorative patterns of peacocks, dragon fish, double dragons, and double phoenixes exhibit a distinct exotic flavoring. Grotto number one is the most special, with its roof fashioned like a mandala. The roof of the adjacent grotto number two is a mandala with five concentric circles. There are 108 Buddha images on the walls on either side of its southern gate, 164 on the northern wall and 308 on each of the eastern and western walls. These grottos share a lot in common with the Dunhuang Mogao grottos.

To better protect the Tunggar-Piyang ruins, the government of Tibet

Autonomous Region kicked off a preservation and restoration project in April 2013. By April of the next year, the first phase of mountain drainage and cave treatment work was finally completed with a total investment of 9.06 million yuan. The second phase of the restoration project is set to start soon.

Many sources have stated that the Tunggar-Piyang ruins were the greatest collection of Buddhist grotto relics ever discovered in China and that this particular set was discovered in 1992. However, the head of the Tunggar village committee, Ngawang, has been guarding the Tunggar grotto relics for over 30 years.

Ngawang is 74 years old. His father passed away when he was very young, so everything fell squarely on his shoulders. In 1959, after the democratic reform of Tibet, he was considered bright and capable by the county and town officials and appointed chief of this village close to the Chinese-Indian border. Ngawang's job keeps him very busy. On the one hand, he is the local village administrator, while on the other hand, he is involved in big construction projects like building roads and canals; he is the link between the construction team and the village. Now, the families in the village all have new houses and a significant number of yaks and sheep, and some have even purchased small tractors. The village is less than 20 kilometers from the asphalt road connecting Bar and Zanda, so it is much easier now for the villagers to go to the county seat.

Ngawang is also responsible for guarding the Tunggar cave. For the past 30 years, he has been taking care of this treasure trove of Tibet. He told us, "Before 1966, villagers often came here to worship, but it was later damaged by some people." To block out people coveting the treasures inside, he secretly made some makeshift doors. Since 1978, the Tunggar grottos have been left unguarded and without a solid gate. To protect the frescos in the cave, Ngawang often goes there by himself to check and make sure everything is in order.

It is a 30-minute walk from the village to the grottos on top of the hills. Since there were no steps, we had to climb along the ditch on the slope. We saw Ngawang's lean frame hobble along and later learned that, for many

Ngawang in the Tunggar grotto.

years, he had suffered from severe arthritis. A couple of years ago, he went to Chengdu to undergo an operation. He said thankfully that the government covered most of his medical bill of 50,000 yuan.

Ngawang might not know the real value of the Tunggar grottos, but he believes that they are a treasure of his hometown and has therefore taken it upon him to guard them. A happy-go-lucky person, he always has a smile on his face when he receives the occasional visitor and gently discourages them from taking pictures. He has received help from both home and abroad, but in order to fundamentally address the issue of Tunggar grotto preservation, it is necessary for the government to intercede.

Ngawang repeatedly took the issue to the county's Administration of Cultural Heritage. In 1998, the government of Tibet Autonomous Region allocated 200,000 yuan to work on the Tunggar grottos, but Ngawang felt that this was far from adequate. Every expert who has been to Tunggar also agrees that they require more comprehensive preservation measures.

Today, Ngawang leads a happy and contented life thanks to the preferential policies of the State. Since Zanda County is located near the border, residents here, including Ngawang, all benefit from border subsidies. In addition to pasture subsidies, residents are further provided with an annual stipend of 7,000 yuan. With the cattle and sheep he raises and the highland barley he grows, Ngawang can now live a comfortable life, but he is not satisfied because he has long harbored a wish to rebuild the temples of Tunggar Village. Still, it is difficult to start such a huge project of several billion yuan in this remote corner of Tibet. To raise money, he even has had some big quarrels with county officials, but he believes that the two temples are the guardian gods of Tunggar and that they will protect both the village and the grottos. When he retires, perhaps there will not be another person like him to guard Tunggar.

Ngawang knows many historical tales by heart. He said that the students of Tsongkhapa had paid a visit to the Tunggar Village temples. He also missed the Phabongkha Monastery in Lhasa and the Ganden Monastery in Taktse County. With few worldly worries, he is in better spirits than ever before. He hopes that the lives of his fellow villagers will continue to get better, and his deepest wish is that the Tunggar grottos, which he has watched for over half a century, will be better preserved and appreciated.

Issue: No.4, 2015.

30

KING GESAR FLOWS ENDLESSLY FROM STONES

— Miraculous Stories of the Female Balladeer Ngodring Droma

Text by Zhou Aiming Photo by Yang Jiaming & Quzha

A call from Professor Yang Jiaming changed my journey to Tibet. Professor Yang advised me that he was going to conduct a field study on the Gesar culture at Seda where there were plentiful Thangkar and rock carvings. He stressed, "The most important thing is that there are several outstanding storytellers of the oral epic *King Gesar*. The first is a monk who can continuously write stories about *King Gesar* from his heart; the second can sing the *King Gesar* stories while begging on the streets… and the third one is the person who could easily sing the stories of *King Gesar* whenever she sees special stones."

I was shocked and surprised. I immediately got permission from my boss and rushed to Chengdu in Sichuan Province. At dawn of the next day, I took the car sent by Seda County government and headed for the Jingma Grassland, where the elevation was about 4,000 meters and the altitude of this grassland is three hundred meters higher than Lhasa.

May and June are the rainy months in the southwest of China. On the way we saw fallen trees and loose rocks on the road because of the previous week's heavy rain. Some rocks blocked three fifths of the road. Fortunately, we got through successfully.

From Chengdu to Seda is about 900-kilometers, but it took us two days in total. We arrived at the downtown of the county and settled down in a hotel by dusk. Surprisingly, I did not have any symptoms of headache or difficulty in breathing while I climbed to the second and third floor. In short, I had no high altitude sickness, and funnily enough… my cold was gone.

Seemingly, King Gesar was giving me his blessing.

My First Meeting with Ngodring Droma

Heading from the downtown of the county, we drove our car on this long journey until we finally arrived before a big yard. The wood-made door on the clay wall was half open. The door was actually propped open by several wood blocks. Sonam Phuntshogs, the deputy director of the Cultural Tourism Bureau of Seda County, told us this was the house of Ngodring Droma.

Striding into the yard, we saw a small well with a water wheel at the southwestern corner of the yard. I tried to some water from the well, while Sonam Phuntshogs shouted for the host of the house. He spoke Amdo dialect that I did not really understand. However, his bawling did not result in any response. With no other choice, we retreated back to the outside of the yard and waited for our host.

In the yard, there was a small green area of flourishing grass that was circled by iron wire and was as high as our knees. One black dog and one white dog lay there silently; apparently they were enjoying basking in the sun because they did not react on seeing us, either by standing up or barking. I guessed they might know Sonam Phuntshogs very well. Suddenly, a woman's voice came from inside. She was Ngodring Droma, an elderly woman.

We presented her with *khada* (white silk scarf) while explaining the purpose of our visit. Director Sonam Phuntshogs helped as our interpreter.

"Do you come from Beijing?" She looked puzzled.

"Yes, we do." I met her gaze directly.

"Do you know the daughter of the Tenth Panchen Lama?" She asked.

"No, I don't know her." I told her honestly. "But the Eleventh Panchen Lama did give me his blessing by touching my forehead."

"Really?" She replied doubtfully.

"Kinchoksum!" I swore confirmation in the Tibetans' fashion.

We stared at each other and finally she smiled happily. The atmosphere became more comfortable. Our young driver, Choedra, relaxed since he had been worried about any embarrassing situation that might happen between us. Ngodring Droma welcomed us to her house.

My Stones Were My Treasures

Ngodring Droma invited us into her house. One bed was placed against each of the southeast and northeast walls. Each was covered with Tibetan cushions. Professor Yang Jiaming invited me to sit in the key seat close to the family altar.

This really WAS an altar, which was built by piling up hundreds of stones of all shapes and sizes. They looked like *Mani* rocks or *Latse*. The sunlight shone directly through a big window, almost as large as the wall itself, into the room and lit up a couple of rocks on which birds, yaks and sheep had been naturally formed. Apparently they were all divine souls depicted in action, either flying or galloping.

"Did you collect all the rocks by yourself?" I asked.

"Yes. All are my treasures!" Ngodring Droma answered seriously. "I love rocks, No matter where I look, I pick them up without caring how dirty it is if I like it. I often lick it to make it clean. And then I check its shape. I believe that these rocks have a profound message about King Gesar. I love rocks because they imply a tremendous number of legends and myths," she said.

Ngodring Droma has loved to collect rocks since she was a teenager. Whenever her eyes fell on the grassland, as long as she found good rocks, she wanted to take them home. There are very few rocks on the grassland. At the most she could find two or three at a time. And even if she does find a rock, it may be hard to find water to clean it so that she can see its real shape. So Ngodring Droma is accustomed to licking rocks to clean them.

Ngodring Droma maintained this practice throughout her middle age until today when she has become an old lady walking with a stick. Her ongoing search for suitable rocks stretches from the remote Shotar Grassland to the holy Mount Druri situated in the area surrounding the downtown of Seda County.

"Somebody made fun of me by asking what I searched for in the rocks, even though I already have difficultly walking with a stick. They guess I am crazy but I don't think so. I believe in King Gesar and that there are plentiful stories about King Gesar left in these rocks. They are just like a kind of auspicious item and all the implications of this auspiciousness is hidden within them."

"I care a lot about personal hygiene. Look at my house; every room makes your feel comfortable. Nonetheless, I am accustomed to licking rocks. I prefer to check what it is about and what it looks like. So my friends criticized me and my family members also argue that this is a bad habit by saying: 'Nobody in the family ever uses another's bowl (Tibetans customarily use their own bowls when they eat and drink and they never share bowls with any others while eating and drinking); how can you pick up a rock to lick it even though sometimes it has touched the shit of dogs!?'"

Ngodring Droma said that no matter how others looked down on her habit; she could not refrain from doing it. She likes to do whatever she likes to do: picking up rocks from a mountain or studying her rocks.

"Look at this one, it has the stamp of Padmasambhava." She took out a small cloth-made bag in which a red rock like an ink stone covered with several *Pulu* textures. She blew on the rock and took it to stamp on the *Pulu* texture. Immediately, a clear stamp print appeared on the surface.

"Is this your favorite rock?"

"This is a treasure, as precious as gold."

"It seems every rock is your treasure!"

"Of course, all of these are from 40–50 thousand years ago during the period of the Ling Kingdom (which was found by King Gesar). They are not dug up from the ground."

She spoke as if she was educating a puzzled student.

"Do you go everyday to pick up rocks?"

"Not actually to pick them up, but rather I would like to say it is the karma between me and the rocks."

As if she had caught me out, she emphasized that finding such treasures was not an everyday opportunity and the real question was whether or not it was *karma*. If so, the treasures immediately appeared in front of the seeker. Otherwise, they could not be found.

"Several years ago, some eminent monks and scholars involved in the study of King Gesar culture gathered on the Seda Grassland. I also went to there to join in. Somebody told me that there was a big rock on the mountainside. It looked like a helmet and was very big. I certainly couldn't move it alone and there were only a few other people. I consulted several Buddhist incarnates but they told me nothing concerning whether or not I was allowed to move it back home. Nonetheless, I believed this was the helmet of King Gesar or somebody who was important to him."

"Are all rocks about King Gesar?"

"Of course, messages about King Gesar are written on these rocks. If there was *karma*, you two could go with me to Mount Druri where there were tremendous relics of King Gesar. On the way, we can talk. Though I cannot move easily, I can take a slow walk and give you a lot of information about King Gesar."

The Incarnate of the Daughter of Chaotong

"Looking at these rocks, they are the *Wirma* of King Gesar (The 13 animals of King Gesar are all named *Wirma* in Tibetan), including roc, wolf, eagle and others. This is the horse whip of King Gesar."

Ngodring Droma solemnly put on her *Drungsha* which was a hat worn especially by the bards of King Gesar while they are singing. She held aloft a colorful streamer and shook it at us.

"This is the horse whip, if it was made by the Muya Rinpoche by following the rules and regulations of religion, then when shaken, it sounds like a horse neighing. Just like this sound," She said and mimicked the sound of horse neighing. "Nevertheless, this one I made by myself. When I sing *Drung* (in Tibetan inhabited areas, Epic *King Gesar* is universally named *Drung*, implying the stories and legends of King Gesar), the whip sounds like nothing at first." Her voice expressed a little regret but soon she became excited again and talked about her communication with the religious master, Ngoshod.

Master Ngoshod was born in 1939 in Gandro Village of Datse Town in Garze County. He lived like a beggar in the Old Tibet. Occasionally, he would listen to sutra delivered by Buddhist incarnates, which he believed was the happiest event in his life. After the founding of the New China, Master Ngoshod worked as a postman in the early days. During that period of the People's Commune Ngoshod, who was functionally illiterate (knowing very few words) could suddenly write out a story of King Gesar entitled *The Birth of the Hero*. This is a substantial amount of the historical Epic of *King Gesar*, describing how King Gesar came into the human world—the Ling Kingdom—from Heaven.

He kept writing everyday but whenever he finished a paragraph, he automatically stopped and resumed his writing the next day. In total he wrote 160 pages of the stories. Unfortunately, all his writing was later lost.

During the 1980s, he took a vow to become a monk in the Datse Monastery, belonging to the Ningma Sect of Tibetan Buddhism. He lived in a sutra room and did not participate in any religious activities, but rather spent his days writing *Drung* of Epic *King Gesar*. Occasionally, by invitation, he wrote one or two canons of the Ningma Sect sutras. He was named "the hiding master", implying he was writing what was hidden in his heart. In 2008, he took over 20 days to rewrite the story *The Birth of the Hero*. In successive years, he wrote out several other stories, including *Sai Ma Den Wei* (Enthronement by horse race), *Pu Ming Ran Den* (Enlighten), and *Xiang*

Fu Hei Peng (Conquer the black roc) and several canons of the Ningma Sect sutras. People invited him to keep on writing, but he refused by saying he had already become an aged man and had accomplished five *Drung*. He commented that such attainments were enough for his life. When we paid him a visit, he said modestly that he was a common man and could not achieved greatness, but he was willing to present his writing of *Drung* to me, and agreed that I take them for future translation into Chinese and English for publication.

After moving to the downtown, Ngodring Droma was willing to pay a visit to Master Ngoshod. They both liked to joke with each other.

"Master Ngoshod says I am the daughter of Chaotong. People say he is a Buddhist incarnate. I guess he is the incarnate of Michung Khade, a figure in *Drong* who has a nimble tongue. Seemingly, he does not dispute what I say. We both like to make a joke sometimes. For instance, we asked when it was the period of the Ling Kingdom and how his family was connected with my family."

In the Epic *King Gesar*, Chaotong is the uncle of King Gesar, who has a vicious mind and heart. He likes making conspiracies. His wife, Sertsodring, delivered ten children to him. Four out of nine boys became well known as heroes in the Ling Kingdom. His daughter Tromotso was one of the most beautiful girls in Ling Kingdom with many virtues. Therefore, Ngodring Droma has welcomed the declaration of Ngoshod as the daughter of Chaotong. She observed proudly that not only Master Ngoshod but also other Buddhist incarnates have said she was the real incarnate of the daughter of Chaotong. She feels extremely honored and believes that everything during the period of King Gesar was wonderful. When I asked why she declared that Master Ngoshod was the reincarnate of Michung Khade, Ngodring Droma started to sing *Drung*.

I am the short figured man named Michung, but
I am also called Khade as I am a nimble man.
I am a story bag,

My long story fills about 18 volumes;
My middle length story is about 108 chapters, and
My short stories number more than 29 thousand.

"Ngoshod is skilled at writing the stories of King Gesar. So if he is not Michung Khade, who else would he be?" She stared at us as if she was debating with us.

"You are almost intoxicated with King Gesar! Do you find a husband just by looking like King Gesar?"

"No, no, no...!"

Her eyes flashed while she was constantly wringing her hands, and then she burst out laughing. When she stopped, she said: "I do like King Gesar, and my husband does not look like King Gesar. On contrary, he is a slim, short man and nowadays we have separated."

We did not get chance to meet the husband of Ngodring Droma. Director Sonam Phuntshogs mentioned that about 11 years ago (1998), Ngodring Droma and her husband moved from the nomadic village of Shotar, which is a very remote area in Seda, to the suburb of the downtown of the county where they built a yard and house. They had four sons and four daughters. It was after this move that Ngodring Droma became completely addict to rocks and could recite *Drung* using her observation of rocks. She spent all day, every day, looking for rocks that were piled up in her house. The house was almost full without any spare space. Thus, her husband built a booth in their yard with wooden shelves set up so that she could store her rocks. One layer after another, she kept collecting and storing them while she assumed that her husband was supporting her habit, although some people, including some of her family members, criticized her. She continued to be totally addicted to collecting until one day her husband had an affair with another woman. She had to separate from him. Her husband moved out and he gave her some *Tsampa* each month. She lived by herself. Nonetheless, her rock collection constantly increased while her *Drung* was also increasing. She started to become well known in the neighboring area and gradually many famous scholars began to pay visits to her.

On hearing this, I felt sad but also respectful. Immediately, I took out 300 yuan and gave it to her. As I had another appointment, I had to say goodbye and promised to come back once again after one or two days. She said she was looking forward to my next visit.

King Gesar in the Eyes of a Teenager

In the next couple of days, we interviewed Yiqiong who was just like a living dictionary of the Gesar culture in Seda. Then we drove to the neighboring Druchen Monastery in Qinghai to interview the Tarluo Rinpoche who was the founder of the Gesar Tibetan Opera Group of Seda County. We traveled to the grassland to photograph the paintings and statues of King Gesar and took our time in the local cultural center to watch and study what they had collected from manuscripts of King Gesar, relics and wood statues of the thirty key high-ranking officers of King Gesar, which were created by Pema Qiao and Yiqiong cooperatively...

On the way, we kept searching for Tupten, a blind bard. It was said that these days he went to a nomadic area to sing the Epic *King Gesar* because herdsmen believed that his singing could bring them the blessing of King Gesar. He believed that he could help the nomads overcome their difficulties and loneliness, and in return Tupten could be offered butter, milk dregs or sometimes a sheep. Tupten is just like Homer living a thousand years ago who could live off his singing. We repeatedly tried to contact him so that he could close his traveling and singing on the wide grassland and return to the downtown as soon as possible. Nonetheless, we had to wait for his coming.

A student of a middle school unexpectedly gives us a big surprise

On that day, we drove a car rapidly up a mountain road to visit the Tarluo Rinpoche. Director Sonam Phuntshogs brought his elder sister's two sons to travel with us. On the way, the two boys sat there silently just like two adults. After arriving at our destination we started to talk with the Tarluo Rinpoche the big boy suddenly opened his mouth, which really surprised us.

The 70-year-old Tarluo Rinpoche was apparently fond of him and started a conversation with him.

His name is Lhagya Tsering, a student of a senior middle school. He believes that where he lives in Seda is the residence of the tribes of the Ling Kingdom. Due to the protection and blessing of King Gesar, great bards and masters have made this land more beautiful and mysteriousness. Regarding the Gesar culture in Seda, Lhagya Tsering concluded as follows:

> King Gesar is not a divinity, but rather a divine hero. In history, there was a hero like this during the period of Ling Kingdom. Due to the reverence and love of the locals, he became a divinity in the heart of the locals, and thus the longest epic in the world was formed. That is *King Gesar*.
>
> From my point of view, Gesar is a divinity. He represents us Tibetans, including our wisdom, bravery and selflessness... Epic *King Gesar* expresses Tibetans in pursuit of peace, consolation, a good life, the prosperity of religion and the people's wishes. That is the reason the Epic *King Gesar* survives so well. In that land of blue skies and white clouds above the extensive grassland, the great epic is passing on from generation to generation...

An Auspicious Day

Two days later, we returned to the house of Ngodring Droma. A small blue *Auto* brand car was parked in the yard but we could not see the owner. Director Sonam called her name and then Ngodring Droma slowly walked out.

"Today is my meditation day. Nevertheless, now you are already here, please come in!"

Once again walking into her small living room, Professor Yang suddenly cried out. “Aiyaya… What auspiciousness! It is definitely an auspicious day. You see, the buttered flowers are blooming!”

On a small table, two butter lamps on a colorful plate were blooming with “butter flowers”. Often, when a butter flower bursts naturally from butter lamp it is recognized as an auspicious sign. I used to watching them as a child, but this was the first time I saw double butter flowers. Interestingly, Professor Yang had given me a cooked egg that looked like a “Nyida”, an image of the overlapping of the moon and the sun according to Tibetan customs. This coincidence surprised Professor Yang!

On my way there, I had told Professor Yang and Sonam my thoughts regarding my proposed report on Ngodring Droma. They both approved of my proposal and Professor Yang promised to shoot a picture for my cover page. On observing this lamp flower, he immediately discussed it with Ngodring Droma in conjunction with presenting our journal to her. He said that her picture would be used as the cover page so that people around the world could get to know her.

Remaining silent for a while (maybe that was her way to ask permission

The collected stones of Ngodring Droma.

of King Gesar), Ngodring Droma finally smiled and agreed to his proposal. "What am I going to wear?" She said and habitually stuck out her tongue. Not waiting for our response, she picked up the door curtain and invited us to come inside saying, "Shoot it, and shoot whatever you want. You folks want these photos, don't you?"

Professor Yang stepped in and turned around to warn me this was an altar and photography was not allowed. I knew only family members and visiting clergymen used the altars of Tibetan families. Now the host had agreed to let us in and as I was physically clean, why couldn't I take a look?

The family altar of Ngodring Droma was surrounded with Thangka related to King Gesar, but I did not see a shrine or any single Buddhist statue. There was a bed on the south side of the room and Thangka paintings hanging on the wall. A small recorder playing a man's voice echoed around the room. I could not recognize who was singing the Epic *King Gesar*. I looked around the room but did not find the knife that her grandson mentioned to me in my last visit. He had said to me: "My grandmother has a knife which was used by King Gesar. She never allows me to touch it!" Of course, such treasures must be stored carefully. So I felt reluctant to mention it. Therefore, I came down to earth by taking a look at the small Thangka paintings and exclaimed:

"Professor Yang, do you believe they are all about *Drungthang*?"

Following my voice, Professor Yang returned inside and examined the Thangka paintings with me. He said he had already collected a little Thangka painting like this small piece here, but he didn't have the second and third one, which he believed he never had seen before. These two included an especially vivid painting of King Gesar and his general officers. Interestingly, every portrait in these two Thangka paintings was captioned with their Tibetan names. One, in particular, Ngodring Droma declared was produced during the period of the "people's commune" when she asked a painter to produce it for her. This was 45 years ago and was unique all over the Tibetan-inhabited area. This information made Professor Yang really excited and he declared the trip worthwhile.

"This can be seen as the reward of King Gesar to you because of the karma between you two," said I with smile.

"Ou Ya! Ou Ya!" Professor Yang shouted in his mother tongue as he was jumping for joy.

Gendun Norbu Geng Jiang

Ngodring Droma put on her clothes one after another and finally, before she put on *Drungsha*, she stuck out her tongue and said: "Do I have to comb my hair?" She did not wait for our response as she had already undone her pigtails and carefully combed her hair. After combing, she wet her fingers and then smoothed down the ends of her hair. I was impressed that she had such deeply dark hair and was especially surprised at her method of combing her pigtails. She did it naturally but occasionally showed her embarrassment by smiling.

After the combing she asked, "Which hat do I put on?" with one hand on her head. Next she walked into the yard to open the fence door. Driver Quzha brought a chair for her and placed it on the grassland, right in front of the big stone booth. We followed her there. The two dogs inside lazily opened their eyes to look at their master, stretched their bodies and then resumed their

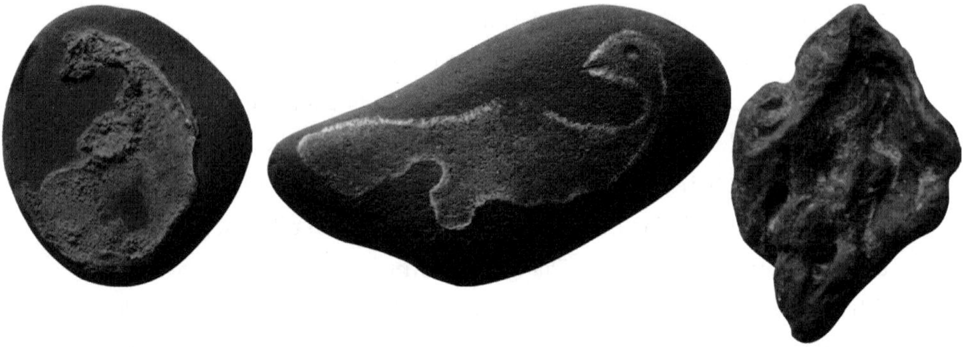

joyful basking in the sunlight.

Ngodring Droma sorted out her clothes and sat down peacefully. Her right hand held a horsewhip and the left hand a black stone. Then she commenced singing.

"This is the mother of King Gesar who comes from the place where the Dragon King is living. The Dragon King gives his lovely daughter a treasure called Gendun Norbu Geng Jiang (meaning whatever a person wants, this treasure will come to him/her at once). The Dragon King says that the seeds planted in summer (spring) will be harvested in autumn and the son of the divinity—Gesar—is going to be born."

"The Dragon King, Dzongna Renchen, is unwilling to let his daughter (Gyamo) marry Ling Kingdom. But Padmasambhava requests that the incarnate of Gesar descend to the human world from Heaven. Thereby, Gyamo is selected as the birth mother of Gesar to descend from the kingdom of Dragons to the Tribe Gya of the human world. When the first battle between Tribe Gya and the Ling Kingdom began, all of the Tribe Gya ran away; only Gyamo remained. She had loaded lots of possessions on the back of a female yak and was ready to run away, but she failed to escape; instead, soldiers from the Ling Kingdom captured her.

"Why did this happen? Before Gesar was sent to the human world, he had made a request to his parents (She started to sing)."

If you grant me;
The father is from Heaven, and
The mother is from the Kingdom of Dragons.
The war horse can understand human words, and
I can descend to the human world.

"Jueru, the son of the divinity, said so. Gyamo's father is the king of the Dragon Kingdom. Dzongna Renchen worries that the princess will have difficulties in the human world. He therefore throws a large amount of treasures into the sea, including stones that are usually used for books of divination. But I failed to find them. There is the place where the dices were thrown. Would you like me to point to you?"

Ngodring Droma closed her eyes while she sang or spoke. Suddenly, she opened her eyes and declared, "It is unnecessary and we all know." Director Sonam immediately interrupted her as he wanted her to continue "Drung" speaking.

Ngodring Droma therefore continued singing with her eyes closed.

"A soothsayer, Tongkhor Gyalpa, came from Heaven. He carried about 500 mules with divination books on their backs while descending from Heaven. He is throwing dices there and people are asking what the situation is."

Ngodring Droma's collectings.

The soothsayer from Heaven—Tongkhor Lha,
The undefiled Buddhist beads at Gerlha
What knots in your hands?
Taking 360 days to count,
Please throw this dice today, and
Today you come to undo the divination.
Tightening the knots one after another,
This is our divination.

"The knot is a line connecting four to five pearls. In total there are four knots. In line with the divination, Padmasambhava is asked to pay a visit to Heaven and the people in Heaven request the poor must be released from poverty and vicious persons must be punished. What should we do? Padmasambhava finishes his sermon, and listeners offer him gold and silver treasures including Gendun Norbu Geng Jiang, but he refuses. He prefers to have the second daughter of King Dragon Gojiang Gyamo. Amongst the three daughters of King Dragon the eldest is Asi Chikyi Nyibum and the third one is Yaga Chiden. This is quite bizarre, why a lama need a wife? It was at this time the Ling Kingdom was founded. Padmasambhava let Gojiang Gyamo descended into the family of Gya Dongpa Gyaltsen. The conflict between Gya and the Ling Kingdom resulted in the Ling Kingdom conquering the 18 tribes of Gya. Gyamo was captured and later Jueru was given a birth…"

Ngodring Droma looked up slightly, seeming to enjoy the sun on the over 4000-meter high land. She kept singing and occasionally she opened her eyes and asked us if it was necessary to change hats. "In fact, she has two hats," Quzha told Professor Yang and then Professor Yang came to question me: "if there were two, why don't we let her try another one?" She changed the hat and resumed her singing. Once, she even waved her hand to call on me to have a photo together with her. Immediately, I sat by her with my handbag. She touched my hair and said: "Zha Zha…You're getting white hair."

"Yes, I do. You don't have any. Can you speak Chinese?!"

"No, I cannot. Maybe couple of words." She smiled again. "Do you have children?"

"Yes, a son. And I heard that you have four sons and four daughters, don't you?"

Speaking of her children, she had a big smile and the deep winkles on her face showed her pride and happiness as a mother.

Gendun Norbu Geng Jiang, who was given up by Padmasambhava, descended to Ngodring Droma's hands after centuries. She was granted the capability of telling "Drung" in conjunction with enjoying a life of many children around her. Today, these children are busy either with their own business or for grazing. As a mother, she feels content.

The Celebrated in Miracles

Ngodring Droma had the sign of the pig in her zodiac at her birth in 1947. Her father Danlho and mother Dachen both came from Shiqu County and immigrated to Chota Village of Seda County in Sichuan Province that then belonged to nomads.

In her childhood, Ngodring Droma did not get a chance for schooling. She was illiterate, but she was fond of hearing others singing oral Epic *King Gesar* "Drung". She remembered the neighboring Polha (Tibetan, meaning "grandpa") had a bizarre hat. He liked to hold this hat while singing "The Eulogy of the Hat". Whenever he opened his mouth to sing, cattle and sheep almost forgot to eat grass, birds forgot to extend their wings to fly and villagers automatically stopped their farming labors to surround him and listen to his singing for three days and nights. At the end of the singing, villagers presented *khada*, butter and *Tsampa* to him. They wanted to give him whatever they had in their hands. Such scenes made the little Ngodring Droma wonder if she could sing "Drung", it could be wonderful! Looking at the white scarf… if it could be put on her neck, it would be beautiful!

One day as she came back from grazing, she picked up a little stone. In the sunlight, it looked like a white conch shining with different colors. Suddenly, she seemed to see people in battle and again many people on horseback. She asked herself, was he King Gesar? That night, she dreamed of King Gesar and seemingly he told her something, but unfortunately she could not remember it after waking up.

Since then, she has been addicted to stones, especially beautiful ones. She brought them home. She believes those stones are the general officers of King Gesar. This was his *Wirma* and her *Dromo*… At times, one or two "Drung" suddenly emerge in her mind but just as she is ready to speak them out they have all gone.

In 1998, she and her husband moved to resettle in the suburbs of the Seda County seat. Since then she has collected more and more stones which all have a very special shapes. The more people she gets in touch with, the more the sentences flowing from her mouth. The sentences naturally connect with one another and finally she starts to sing "Drung". Some people say she has gone crazy and others think of her as being under an illusion. She, however, believes this is the "Drung" which the mighty King Gesar grants to her. She positively asserts she is fully mentally aware and that her singing is "Drung". The experts and Tibetan Buddhist Rinpoches from the county level also recognize her singing as "Drung".

"This one was got when King Gesar conquered Ser Dzong of Ngari. This is the footprint of his war-horse and these are the footprints of Jueru. This is the throne of King Gesar." She introduced all her treasures and then ushered us to a pile of stones placed on a table outside of the big booth in which her stones were preserved. She endlessly counted out her treasure stones. At this moment, the horsewhip that could sound like neighing of horses became her teaching pointer.

"This is the soul stone of Chaotong. Look, it is on this one that there is a round sign. This is a stone for the Medicine King. Originally, Mewa Chingmu Rinpoche said he would come to pick it up on the 15th of this month. He is fond of smoking and sometimes he tells lies, but he is indeed a great incarnate."

"My stones were also gifted to Chockyi Gyatso Rinpoche. He was very pleased and asked me if this stone was my medical bag. I guessed if I gave him the stone (looking like a medical bag) he might think he would get sick and unhappy. Therefore, I answered that this was the medical bag made by Sakyamuni when he produced *Duetsi* (nectar). I said this one could cure all kinds of diseases occurring in all kinds of worlds, including those diseases that doctors might not have any method to cure. On hearing this, the Rinpoche delightfully accepted the medical-bag stone. After a time, he designated a person to tell me that medical bag really played an important role in curing his recent sickness.

"Mt. Senggong Puzhuri (the mountain's name in Seda) has footprints of the war-horses of King Gesar on its side. Descending further it is Serko and there is the castle of Nyibong Daya where there are plentiful ruins of the King Gesar era. Many people know this. All that I am feeling comes naturally. It just like what I sing. What is truth? People say I am mad, but I disagree. Nonetheless, if I can speak for myself, you'd better write down my words. If an old person like me can tell you lies, you might believe there was nothing worth taking away. My children ridicule me and they guess what I named the stones and make up stories about them. Notwithstanding, I believe that 'Drung' is coming from these stones and I just sing them out."

"Occasionally, I am probably capable of being a talkative person, but at times when I should speak out I fail to do so since my feeling was not there at that particular moment. For instance, twice when you came here, my words were welled up without stopping, which really made me feel excited and I believe you may be sick of me."

"The purpose of our visit is to listen to your singing and speaking of 'Drung'," We replied, "Of course, we would like you to sing and speak as long as possible."

I dreamed maybe one day we could invite her to sing in the inland or overseas so that people could witness the miracle. I asked her: "You are used to speaking and singing at home while watching stones. How would this be possible if you were outside of your home?" She replied happily, "It is no problems at all. I am an ordinary person, but the stones and 'Drung' are the 'be and end-all' of my life."

Seven years ago, Ngodring Droma formally acknowledged Tsering Lodro as her master. She followed him to be vegetarian. Apart from having a problem with bone hyperplasia, she has a very fit body. Her master convinced her to have a meditation at times. Though she could not completely isolate herself in a cave, just like a nun, she follows his suggestion. Nonetheless, she did not refuse us when we encountered her during her meditation.

We could not precisely count her stones and of course hardly have time to listen to all her stories about the stones. Even so, nobody can really deny her stones are treasures. As for the oral epic King Gesar, questions like how long does it go? How profound is its content and how many of the stories are included? Those who have a Karmic relationship with this epic can only answer these questions.

Before setting off, Ngodring Droma took a small amount of beads from a small table. Then she took out a thread and tried to push it through the beads. However, the thread was too soft and it would not go through. She tried using a matchstick and also burnt the end of the thread, but ultimately this failed. I took out my sewing bag from my travel pack and threaded a needle with the thread. My efforts at forcing a needle to go through the zigzagging beads holes were a total failure. She laughed at me, snatched it away and then kept trying her original method. Finally, she had success, she made a necklace. She looked at me and took a big bow, saying: "Look, I have magic."

We all burst into laughter at this.

Director Sonam took hold of the necklace and passed it to me: "She wants you to have this as a gift!"

I was surprised. Maybe my mouth was open wide and everybody laughed at me. Ngodring Droma extended her hands to touch my head, just like a benevolent mother caressing her daughter. She was actually giving me a blessing. She came outside with us and said farewell while bowing her head to touch my head.

"This *Ama* (Tibetan, meaning "mother") is the most celebrated of the miracles!" Quzha said this while his one hand was steering the car and the other hand was waving to say farewell to Ngodring Droma.

I looked back at her bowed body standing there firmly outside of her yard as her figure gradually became smaller and smaller. It seemed like she would never turn her back before our vehicles were out of sight. I silently prayed for her: worshiping King Gesar!

I prayed Ngodring Droma would have auspicious days and nights and wished her legend be disseminated to every corner of the world!

Issue: No.2, No.3, 2011.

31
TRUE HEROES

Text by Liang Xvchang

Each year, I spend six months in a place with an average altitude of 5,000 meters above sea level. Its name? Changtang.

Changtang is one of the most sparsely populated areas in the world. Boasting the largest plateau grassland ecosystem on Earth, it is one of the few paradises of wild animals remaining. 80 percent of the world population of Tibetan antelopes and wild yaks can be found here, and a large number of large carnivores, including brown bears, snow leopards, and wolves, are also widely distributed here.

As a wildlife professional, my job consists of two parts: the outdoors and the indoors. What I like most about this job is that it provides me with balanced opportunities to develop both intellectually and physically; it is also one of the few careers in the world that can take you deep into forests and mountains to explore the magnificence of nature.

Though I often work in harsh conditions, such as how I track herds of wild animals all by myself, it is not without a subtle yet ceaseless sense of excitement.

Years ago, I made an impulsive decision to devote my life to the cause of wildlife conservation, but when I look back, I honestly see now how I just wanted to be a hero then, to be someone admired by others in a cause that sounded a bit idyllic to me.

To be the hero I wanted to be, I visited many places in Changtang and

Dr. George Schaller. Photo by Kang Aili

dreamed of living like a 19th-century field biologist, which to me was the ultimate definition of "cool". To get a good view of some wild yaks, I once got lost on a freezing stormy night, and while monitoring snow leopards, I had a close encounter with a roaring brown bear. I even drew up a travel plan with some friends. We were determined to go the ancient style: packing a couple of yaks, leading them across the wilderness of Changtang, and walking alongside wild animals.

However, the novelty eventually faded. Compared with the hero figures in my imagination, I felt I was lacking in some respects. This feeling of frustration reached its zenith in May of 2013, when a colleague and I untangled a pregnant female Tibetan antelope from the fences. Its neck was trapped in the wires, and it soon died right in front of us, its body still warm. Two days later, its carcass had been eaten by vultures and crows.

I began to question if I had really done anything to advance the cause of wildlife conservation or if I were merely chasing an unrealistic fantasy.

Poachers used to be a big threat to Tibetan antelopes. Now they are being fended off and cracked down on. Even when compared to other areas around the world, Changtang National Nature Reserve is one of the best administered, but environmentally speaking, it is one of the fastest warming areas in the world. The temperature is climbing at a rate twice that of the average global figures, and the quantity, quality, and distribution of its ecological resources are changing profoundly and rapidly. In the second half of the 20th century, human activities expanded almost 200 kilometers toward the depopulated zone in the north; the web of roads has been getting denser by the year; and long fences have begun to be built on the fertile grasslands. The wild animals' access to water and food has been restricted, with their migration patterns being disrupted sometimes.

Every year for the past 200 million years, an average of one vertebrate species would die out, and every 27 years, a higher plant species. Nowadays, it is estimated that 75 species vanish every day. By 2050, a quarter of the species now roaming on Earth may not exist anymore. We are in the middle of the sixth mass extinction in the history of evolution. Humans are the main reason behind this. Countless species of wildlife had stood the test of time for millions of years but have been perishing in front of our eyes.

In these circumstances, how could I possibly become a genuine hero who does what is truly best for wild animals? Time and tide wait for no one. I pondered this for quite a while.

So it was until I met three particular men.

The first one I will mention here is Norbu Dradul, a low-ranking government official in Tsonyi County in northern Tibet. The township he works in lies at an average altitude of 4,800 meters above sea level and has a total land area of over 10,000 square kilometers. Its population, however, is less than 2,000. Norbu is a natural-born animal lover. For some years, when he had some free time on weekends, he would voluntarily accompany me on my research trips.

At that time, I had a rather low opinion of humans. I believed that people had a duty to live harmoniously with and have an inherent affection toward

The herdsmen wildlife protectors, the man of right one is Tagye.

wild animals, with pasture fences best taken down and banned. Every day after work, Norbu Dradul and I would chat over our dinner of roasted lamb legs. "We stopped hunting a long time ago," he would say, "but brown bears, snow leopards, and wolves, they attack cattle and sheep and damage houses. How can you possibly expect people to have a genuine passion and liking for wild animals?"

One time, he asked me, "You hate pasture fences, but without them, the grass would all be eaten away by kiangs and antelopes. Domestic animals would starve to death. You are a wildlife conservation professional; you get paid for this! We are just ordinary farmers and herdsmen whose livelihood relies on the livestock. What can we be expected to do?"

As a grass-roots community leader, Norbu Dradul is usually very busy. I often see him doze off holding a cup of butter tea at night, completely exhausted. To help his fellow villagers lift themselves out of poverty, he encourages herders to form cooperative societies and draws up concrete plans for them. After disasters caused from snowfall, he visits all the settlements affected and delivers relief supplies to residents. During such times, roads can be perilous. He even fought off a brown bear once with his bare hands. He told me that he was afraid of neither Heaven nor Earth; what he did fear was letting his people down and failing in his duties.

Humans are so powerful now that they can wipe out any species if they should ever want to, but Norbu Dradul and his fellow townsfolk would not agree with such a statement. They feel they are the disadvantaged group in this competition for existence against wild animals. In these remote places with harsh living conditions, it is by no means easy to make a living. The abundance of wild animals adds more trouble to their already difficult lives. To them, wild animals are often thieves, bandits, or even killers. Last year, a herdsman in Norbu Dradul's township was killed in a tragic incident involving a brown bear.

Norbu Dradul helped me realize two things: first, these decent, hardworking people are in no way the nemeses of wildlife conservation. It is true that they are competing for limited natural resources against wild animals, but that is not their fault. They have rights, every bit as much as the local animals, to seek a safe and comfortable life. Second, if wildlife conservation professionals do not respect this first point, their jobs will be doomed.

Despite all his arguments, in 2014, during the migration season of Tibetan antelopes, Norbu Dradul came to me hurriedly, saying he had seen 200-plus Tibetan antelopes trapped in a fenced-in area. "I can't deal with this anymore, bro," he finally said to me, "These antelopes are too miserable. Let's cut the fences open and set them free." From then on, he continued to do the same thing every year.

The second person I want to mention is named Tagye. A couple of years ago, we did a population survey on snow leopards in his hometown of Shantsa County. Tagye and several friends of his acted as our field guides. Across several months, we ate, lived, and worked together. A close camaraderie often found among field workers soon formed among us. They started as road guides but gradually learned to design snow leopard population surveys, read a geographic coordinate system, and use infrared cameras.

Later, when we came to know each other well, Tagye said to me, "When I was little, the village elders told me that the wild animals were our brothers living in the mountains. I neglected my brothers in the past; it's about time I began helping them."

As part-time wildlife rangers hired by the forestry authority of the autonomous region, today, Tagye and his colleagues spend six months every year to perform scientific monitoring of snow leopards and patrol their habitat. They also made a short video using footage captured by infrared cameras and showed it to villagers to raise awareness on wildlife conservation. Recently, the group has been planning a series of events under the guidance of the county forest bureau. First, they are turning their village into the first administrative village in Tibet to implement "proactive protection measures against beasts of prey". They also hope that their hometown, in two years' time, will become the first "community wild animal protection area" in Tibet.

Out of courtesy and respect, Tagye and his buddies always call me "professor", but in my heart, they have long been my own teachers. I cannot remember how many times I have watched them climb onto snow-covered cliffs and leap over fear—inducing ditches to meticulously perform their tasks. Once their work is done, they always find a patch of grass under the sun and start playing around and messing with each other.

I respect these young men from the bottom of my heart, not only because of their stamina, which I could never dream of having, but their mindset: they see wildlife conservation as a way of life, as natural as eating and sleeping.

They do not seem to have any distractions, something that humbles me to my core.

The third man is a prominent figure in wildlife conservation: 85-year-old Dr. George Schaller, whom *Time Magazine* named as one of the top three field biologists of the 20th century.

Dr. Schaller has worked in his area of study for more than 50 years, producing a prolific body of works and setting a great example for generations of younger scientists to follow. In 2016, at a campsite under a

Norbu Dradul (Left 1) is studying how to use GPS for coordinates.

temperature of negative 20 degrees Celsius, I asked him to talk about himself and his achievements. His answer was surprisingly solemn, "I am now lying in an ice-cold tent, as I have been doing over several decades. What have I achieved? The voice in my head always points out my failures. I have not accomplished anything: I have not founded any conservation organization; I do not teach in a university; I have not put forward significant new theories, and I have no new ground-breaking thoughts. Except for the great discoveries made by the likes of Isaac Newton, Charles Darwin, and Albert Einstein, most scientific achievements will soon be replaced and forgotten. Mine are no different. At most, they will provide minor reference points for future studies."

I was speechless. This was not what I expected.

"How can you say that?" I protested. "Where's the light at the end of the tunnel?"

He replied with a big smile on his face, "Well, there is still a lot of work to be done in this area. At the very least, observing the complex and colorful lives of other species and trying your best to conserve them is something wonderfully fulfilling."

Last summer, Dr. Schaller visited Tibet again after ten years of being away. He was overjoyed to see how far wildlife conservation efforts have progressed in Changtang with his own eyes. He shook hands with, bowed to, and gave heartfelt thanks to each and every one of us.

In the field of nature conservation, 99 percent of what we see on a daily basis is sad news: one species has gone extinct; another is endangered; etc. From time to time, however, there is that one percent of good news worthy of a good night's sleep.

We are lucky to have that one percent, because many selfless people, such as Norbu Dradul, Tagye, and Dr. Schaller, are making efforts, big and small, to change the world for the better.

They may not have so many lofty aims, like trying to be a hero; they may not be familiar with scientific theories, such as concerning the relationship between humans and animals. What they do have is a strong sense of responsibility, clear actions, and persistence.

Dr. Schaller was so calm and reflective with his words, but he said something heartfelt which resonated with me, "One species is fighting for the survival of other species in the face of huge difficulties. This is unprecedented in the 3.5 billion years of the evolutionary history of life on Earth."

Whenever I think of this, I am filled with pride. It is my great honor to know these amazing individuals and work alongside them. What we have been doing is something unprecedented throughout the past 3.5 billion years. With something as cool as that, there really is no time for heroism!

Issue: No.1, 2019.

POSTSCRIPT

The selected articles in this collection were published during the past 30 years in English edition of *China's Tibet.* It tries to show the economic and social development of Tibet and the improvement of people's life as comprehensively as possible through the historical record of events and life details of typical figures. Most of selected articles are highly recommended or widely praised ones. Unfortunately, some of the authors have passed away, and some of characters in story have departed from us forever. Sincerely, we cherish the memory of them, and take this opportunity, we would like to express our heartfelt gratitude to those who have made contributions to the development of the snow-covered plateau. Being subject to the limits of our ability, inadequacies are unavoidable. Criticisms and feedbacks are really welcomed.

Wang Shuo
Executive Editor-in-Chief

30 Years of Fine Publications *of China's Tibet*

PEOPLE ON THE QINGHAI-TIBET PLATEAU

青藏高原人物

edited by
CHINA'S TIBET MAGAZINE

ISBN 978-7-5211-0199-7
First Published in November, 2019
China Tibetology Publishing House
（中国藏学出版社）
Printed in Beijing, China

图书在版编目(CIP)数据

青藏高原人物 = People on the Qinghai-Tibet Plateau : 英文 / 中国西藏杂志社编 . —北京 : 中国藏学出版社，2019.11

(《中国西藏》杂志 30 年精选集)

ISBN 978-7-5211-0199-7

Ⅰ. ①青… Ⅱ. ①中… Ⅲ. ①人物 – 生平事迹 – 西藏 – 英文 Ⅳ. ① K820.875

中国版本图书馆 CIP 数据核字 (2019) 第 274817 号

青藏高原人物

People on the Qinghai-Tibet Plateau

中国西藏杂志社　编

责任编辑	张荣德
装帧设计	海龙视觉
出版发行	中国藏学出版社
印　　刷	中国电影出版社印刷厂
版　　次	2019 年 11 月第 1 版第 1 次印刷
开　　本	787 毫米 ×1092 毫米　1/16
印　　张	16
字　　数	320 千字
书　　号	ISBN 978-7-5211-0199-7 / K · 572
定　　价	80.00 元

图书如有印装质量问题　请与本社发行部联系

E-mail: dfhw64892902@126.com　电话: 010-64892902